Loving Encounters

A Book For Teenagers About Sex

Loving Encounters

A Book For Teenagers About Sex

Rosemary Stones

Piccadilly Press · London

Phototypeset by York House Typographic Ltd.,
London W7
Printed and bound by Adlard & Son Ltd.,
Letchworth, Herts
for the publishers Piccadilly Press Ltd.,
5 Canfield Place, London NW6 3BT

British Library Cataloguing in Publication Data
Stones, Rosemary
Loving Encounters: a book for teenagers about sex.
I. Sex instruction for youth
I. Title
306.7′024055 HQ35

ISBN 1-85340-005-X

Rosemary Stones. British. She lives in South West London. She wrote *Too Close Encounters: And What To Do About Them*, as well as compiling *More to Life than Mr Right* for Piccadilly Press.

For Andrew

Acknowledgements

Thanks for advice and information to Dr Jennifer Pietroni, Dr William Stones, Margaret Allen of the Lloyd Clinic, Guy's Hospital, Margot Turner and Nigel Pugh of FACT, Andrew Mann of South Bank Family Rights, George Pettifer and John Vincent of Lambeth Amenity Services.

Contents

SECTION 1
BODY CHANGES

The physical changes that transform you, over a number of years, from a child to a young woman or young man are called puberty. The age at which these physical changes start varies from person to person, but generally development takes place between the ages of 9 and 17, with girls tending to develop earlier and faster than boys. Remember though, that everyone is different and everyone will develop at the age and at the rate that is 'correct' for them – the one in fact that has been laid down by their genetic make-up. For example, some girls of 10 have periods, some 16-year-old girls don't yet; some boys have hairy faces at 13, some 18-year-old boys have hardly any hair on their faces. All this is quite normal.

If you live with your biological parents (ie you're not living with adoptive or foster parents), you can get an idea how you are likely to turn out physically by looking at them. If both your biological parents have big feet, for example, you'll probably have big feet. Other factors are also important in physical development. Your weight and the quantity and quality of the food you eat can have an effect on your rate of development. An important influence on your rate of development is whether you feel loved and cared for.

Up to about the age of 8 or 9, girls' and boys' bodies look much the same apart from the sex organs. They are straight up and down with slim shoulders, no waist or hips, flat chests with small nipples and no body hair. Girls' and boys' voices sound the same.

At puberty your body begins to change and develop so that you will be able to have children. Of course this doesn't mean that you *have* to have children – that will be entirely up to you. You can see many of the physical changes that are happening to your body by looking in the mirror, but other changes will be going on too that you can't see. Ways of thinking, feelings and emotions are affected while bodily changes are taking place. Your position in society will be changing too – you're no longer a 'child' but moving towards adulthood. These emotional and social changes are discussed on p. 35 of this book.

Bodily changes for girls and boys begin when the tiny pituitary gland, which is situated just below your brain, starts to produce chemicals called hormones which are released into your bloodstream. These hormones act upon the sex glands so that they begin to grow. In girls these glands are called ovaries and in boys testes or testicles. After a couple of years, the ovaries will begin to send out ova or human eggs and the testes will start to produce sperm, the tiny seeds that can fertilise these eggs. The ovaries and testes also begin to produce sex hormones of their own (different in girls and boys) and these hormones cause sexual changes to take place to the rest of your body.

GIRL INTO WOMAN: FIRST STAGES OF PUBERTY

The onset of puberty for girls usually occurs between the ages of 9 and 15, but for some girls it can be younger and for some older. You will find that:

1. You grow in height. Some girls experience surges of growth and find that none of their clothes fit. They have to get used to suddenly being longer

and bigger. This can make you awkward and clumsy until you get used to it.

2 You grow in weight. You'll probably put on about 12 pounds (5.4 kilograms) before your periods start and another 8 to 12 pounds each year until you reach adult weight. This weight gain is quite normal and does not mean that you are fat. If you think you've a weight problem you should cut down on things like sweets and chips and exercise more but you should consult your doctor before starting any kind of strict diet – it's not always a good idea to diet when you're growing.
3 You're stronger than you used to be.
4 Your hips are wider and fuller.
5 Your face becomes fuller and your voice slightly lower.
6 Your nipples grow larger. Some girls' nipples stick out a lot, some look flat and some are inverted (they look as if they've been pushed in) – all these kinds are quite normal.
7 Your breasts begin to appear. Little pads of tissue develop under the nipples and begin to grow. Some girls notice that their breasts feel tender and they have a tingling feeling. This is to do with growing and it's quite normal. Some girls find that one breast grows faster than the other – this is also normal; you'll find that the other one will catch up eventually.
8 Hair grows over your pubic bone. It is coarser and often darker than the hair on your head. It's called pubic hair.
9 Hair grows under your armpits.
10 You may get dark down hair on your upper lip, a few dark hairs on your chin, an odd hair round your nipples and on your stomach in a line from

your umbilicus (belly button) downwards. You may get hairier legs. All this is very common, especially if the older women in your biological family are hairy people. If you're not happy about it, further on in this book I discuss what to do about it.

11 Your skin and hair get greasier than they used to.
12 You sometimes get a white discharge on your pants from your vagina. This is quite normal and a sign that your periods will start within the next 12 months or so.
13 You have dreams and fantasies about love and sex.

GIRL INTO WOMAN: LATER STAGES OF PUBERTY

Your body will continue to change gradually over a number of years until you are a fully grown woman. You will find that:

1 Your breasts increase in fullness and roundness. You may decide to start wearing a bra.
2 Your pubic hair becomes coarser. Some girls have quite thick pubic hair, others very little. It doesn't matter either way. If it grows so that it shows when you wear a swimsuit, see p 31.
3 You start to have regular periods.
4 You tend to get spots.
5 You sweat more and have to be careful about body odour.
6 The lips of your vulva (the external female sex organs between your legs) grow and become more full.

The Female Sex Organs

On each side of the lower abdomen are the ovaries; these are store-houses for egg-cells or ova. The ovaries release one egg each month, usually alternately. (If eggs are released simultaneously and fertilised it results in non-identical twins.) The egg is drawn along the fallopian tube to the uterus or womb. If the egg is fertilised by a sperm (male sex cell), the resulting embryo attaches to the spongy, blood-rich wall of the uterus (the endometrium) and grows into a baby. If the egg is not fertilised, both it and the endometrium are expelled from the body each month during menstruation (a period). Menstruation begins at puberty and continues until women are about 50. The cervix is the entrance to the uterus. It stays closed unless you have a period, when it opens slightly to let the menstrual blood trickle out. If a baby is ready to be born, the cervix opens fully. The cervix extends into the vagina. The vagina is a highly elastic tube where semen is deposited during vaginal intercourse. The vagina can stretch to allow a baby to be born. Menstrual blood flows down the vagina from the uterus. (If you decide to use a tampon during your periods you push it into your vagina.) It is not possible for things (eg a tampon) to get 'lost' in your vagina or pass into other parts of your body.

The Vulva

The entrance to the vagina is covered by the vulva or external female sex organs, situated between your legs. If you've not already done so, it's a good idea to find out what yours looks like. You will need a mirror, clean hands and some private time to yourself. Sit on the floor with your legs apart and knees bent and prop or hold the mirror so that you can see the area between your legs (your vulva). It consists of two sets of lips, the inner and outer vaginal lips, and looks rather like an unfolding flower. (If you ever get a chance to see Judy Chicago's famous exhibition celebrating women and their history, 'The Dinner Party', you will see that many of the women artists whose work is part of the exhibition have used vulvas to symbolise women and have represented them as unfolding flowers.)

If you look at the diagram on p 11 you will be able to identify the different parts of your vulva: the outer lips (labia majora) protect the inner area and keep it moist. They become covered with pubic hair on the outside. If you gently part the outer lips you will see the inner lips (labia minora); they are two folds of tissue, pinkish or brownish in colour. The inner lips grow during puberty. Some girls have inner lips which stick out beyond the outer ones; some girls have very small inner lips; some girls have one lip longer than the other. All this is quite normal. Like any other part of your body, your vulva is yours and it won't look exactly like anyone else's. At the top of the lips the folds join together to form a hood which covers the clitoris. The clitoris lies in front of the urinary opening (the urethra). You may be able to see the crown of the clitoris – a very sensitive tip of flesh about the size of a pea which is usually hooded when not sexually stimulated. If you put your finger there you will probably have a nice feeling. The clitoris has deeper structures under the skin: the corpus (or body) can be felt with your fingertips just under the surface of the skin; the crura (or legs) cannot be easily felt – they run along the lower part of the pubic bones between the inner thighs. When it is sexually stimulated, the clitoris becomes engorged with blood and swells in the same way that a male's penis becomes erect when sexually aroused.

Vulva – the outer female sex organs

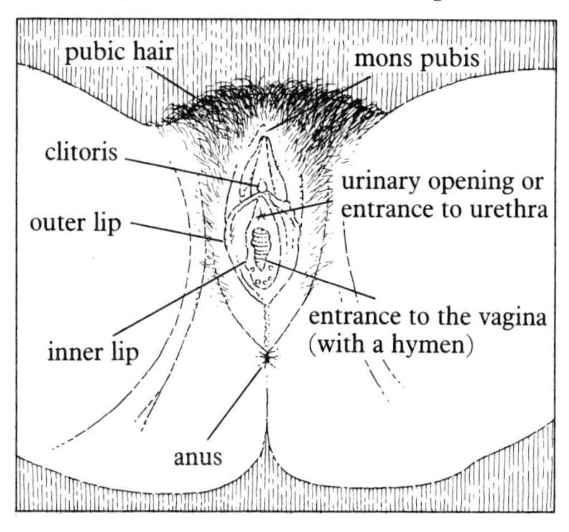

The Urethra

The urinary opening or urethra looks like a tiny dot. Urine (pee) comes out through this opening from a tube from your bladder. The urethral structures also swell when you are sexually aroused.

The Hymen

The opening to your vagina may be partially covered by a thin elastic membrane called the hymen. In the past it was thought that the hymen was broken when a girl or woman first had vaginal intercourse and that a girl/woman without a hymen was therefore not a virgin (someone who has not had sexual intercourse). In fact some girls are born without a hymen and some others break their hymen quite naturally when riding, doing gymnastics etc. You can only stop being a virgin by having sexual intercourse. If you have got a hymen, it will have one or more openings through which menstrual blood can flow when you have your period.

The Mons

The mons is a fatty pad which covers the pubic bone. It is covered with pubic hair.

The Anus

The anus is the opening to the rectum. It is small, strong and has numerous nerve-endings. It holds faeces (shit/turds) in or pushes them out of the body.

The female sex organs

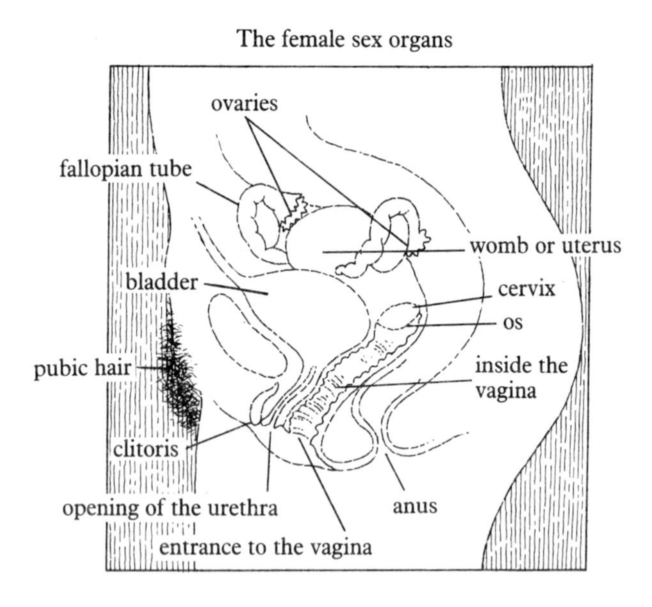

Cervical Smears

All girls and women should be tested at least every three years to make sure that the cells of their cervix are not changing and becoming cancerous. Cancer of the cervix is one of the commonest forms of cancer in women, but unlike most other common cancers, cervical cancer can be prevented by this form of screening. It is particularly important for sexually active girls to be tested – sex does not *cause* cancer but in some cases it can increase a girl's chances of getting it. The test is called a cervical smear. You lie on your back with your legs apart and knees bent. The doctor inserts a speculum (a metal or plastic instrument which holds open the walls of the vagina) and then gently scrapes off a few cells from the cervix with a spatula. This doesn't hurt. The smear is then sent to a laboratory for examination under a microscope to see if there are any cells that may possibly progress to cancer if not treated. Sometimes minor abnormalities are found that need to be observed but not treated. If these abnormalities do need to be treated, a minor operation is carried out to remove the abnormal cells. This does not affect the girl/woman's sex life or her ability to have babies. Cervical cancer is curable if detected early so make sure that you have a cervical smear at least every three years, or sooner if you have any abnormal bleeding or discomfort.

Breasts

Breasts grow in all sorts of different sizes and shapes – if you look at the adult women in your biological family, your breasts are likely to grow something likes theirs. Breasts are made up of fat and milk-producing glands. If you later decide to have a baby, these glands will produce milk to feed it. The baby will suck your nipples to draw out the milk. The size of the breast has nothing to do with the amount of milk it can produce; women with very small breasts are able to feed their baby, if they want to.

In our society, breasts are considered to be erotic objects. Other societies focus on other parts of the body – in Japan, for example, the nape of the neck is considered an erotic area. The models chosen to pose topless in pornographic magazines and tabloid newspapers tend to be women with large prominent breasts. Remember that this is only one kind; there are plenty of others, larger and smaller, and very nice too. If your breasts don't look like the ones on display in the press, it doesn't mean that you're not sexually attractive or not sexy. (Would you want to be fancied anyway by someone who just saw you as a pair of tits?)

Wearing a Bra

Breasts do not have muscle fibres so as women get older their breasts begin to stretch and sag. For this reason many women choose to wear a bra – to prevent the supporting fibres of the breast being stretched. But you don't have to wear a bra if you don't want to – it's up to you.

Girls with large breasts usually find it more comfortable to wear a bra as their breasts can weigh heavily and feel uncomfortable. Lots of girls like to wear a bra for sports so that their breasts are held firmly in place. Wearing or not wearing a bra is really a question of fashion and personal taste.

Breast Cancer: Examining Your Breasts

Cancer of the breast kills more women in Britain than any other form of cancer. Early detection is very important; you should be familiar with the shape, feel and look of your breasts so that if there is any abnormal change you can have it checked by your doctor at once.

The diagram on p 16 shows you how to check your breasts for abnormal lumps or thickening of the tissues. Quite normal breasts contain grainy masses so don't panic when you first do it if yours feel like this. It's often reassuring to ask a doctor to check your breasts the first time and go over with you how to do it so that you can check them yourself in future. The best time to do it is after your period.

If you're the sort of person who, being honest, won't get around to checking your breasts in a systematic way, then you should get into the habit of soaping your breasts in the bath or shower with your hands rather than with a flannel or sponge. You will then automatically be familiar with the normal shape and feel of your breasts and be more likely to detect any changes that need looking into. You should also make a habit of looking at your breasts in a mirror.

Apart from any abnormal lumps or thickening of tissue you should look out for:

- unusual changes in the size or shape of a breast
- discharge from the nipple
- one breast unusually higher or lower than the other
- unusual turning in of the nipple or other changes in its shape
- unusual pain or discomfort

If you discover any of these signs you must go to your doctor at once. In teenagers the problem is far more likely to be a harmless cyst than cancer; but if it is cancerous then it must be treated immediately.

Periods

For the first two years after your periods start, they are likely to be irregular. This is because you are not yet ovulating (releasing an egg). It's a good idea to note in your diary when your periods start and end. Once you

Use the flat of your fingers, gently but firmly feel your breast for any lump or unusual thickening. Start at the inner side and feel around towards the nipple.

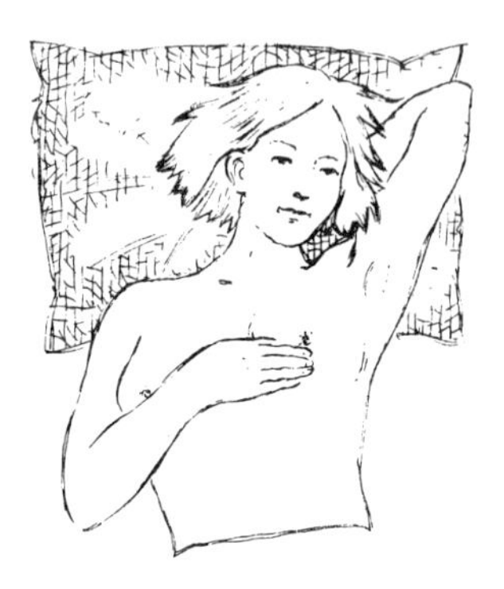

In the same way, examine the lower, inner part. Examine the area all around the nipple too.

Bring your arm to your side as you examine the lower outer part.

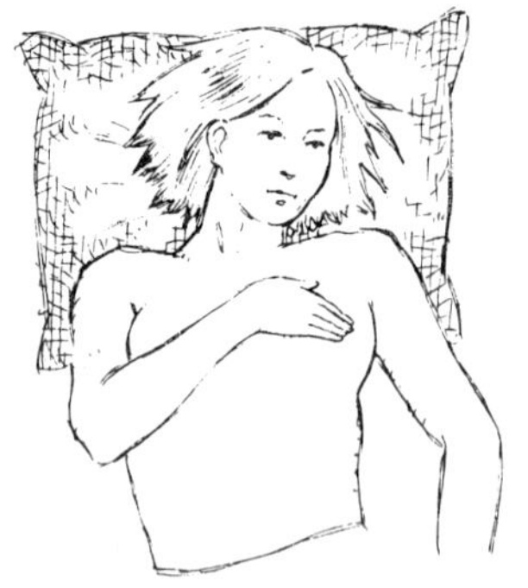

Feel the upper, outer part and then you will have come full circl[e] There is a little extra section of breast tissue between the upper outer part and the armpit, so examine this.

How to examine your breasts for lumps
(This must be done lying down)

begin ovulating, you will see a pattern develop and you will be able to predict when your period will start. Some girls worry that if they miss a period, for whatever reason, the menstrual blood is somehow building up inside them. This is not so.

Periods can last anything from 2-6 days. The time between the start of one period and the next is called the menstrual cycle. This lasts, on average, 28 days, but it can be shorter or longer depending on what's usual for you. It can also be affected if you're feeling tense or anxious about anything. Ovulation (the release of the egg) usually takes place 10-14 days before the start of a period.

Towels and Tampons

When you start having periods you need to use some kind of sanitary protection to absorb the trickle of blood and prevent it staining your clothes.

You can wear sanitary towels (STs) or tampons or a combination of the two depending on how heavy the flow of blood is. Teenage magazines often have advertisements for towels and tampons with coupons for free samples. Before your periods start, it's a good idea to send off for these so that you can decide which kind is best for you. It's also a good idea to compare notes with your friends.

A sanitary towel is a soft absorbent pad with a sticky strip on one side that you can press onto your pants to hold it in place. The towel is shaped so that it is not noticeable, whether you're wearing trousers or a skirt. There are different thicknesses of towels (eg 'regular', 'super', 'mini'). You can wear a thick one at night and during the day when the flow is heavy, and a mini pad when the flow has almost stopped.

Some towels can be flushed down the lavatory but a bulky towel may cause a blockage. In public lavatories there is usually a special bin or incinerator for used sanitary towels. If you're away from home and not sure what to do, roll the used towel up and wrap it around in several layers of lavatory paper until you have a chance to throw it away. If you're throwing used towels into a dustbin, it's best to wrap them in newspaper or in a plastic bag first.

Tampons are finger-sized sticks of hard cotton wool with a cord at the end. You push a tampon into your vagina where it will expand and absorb the flow of blood. When you need to change it (every couple of hours depending on how heavy the flow is), you pull it out by the cord and flush it away. Some tampons have cardboard applicators which make them easier to insert.

Tampons come in different thicknesses (eg 'regular', 'super'), and you choose which to use depending on how heavy the flow is. If the flow is very heavy, or at night, it's sometimes a good idea to use a tampon and a sanitary towel, in case of leaks.

Some girls find it tricky to insert a tampon at first. Sometimes it's because their vagina is rather dry, sometimes it's because they're not sure which direction their vagina goes. It's a good idea to acquaint yourself with your vagina by exploring it gently with clean fingers. Part the lips of the vulva and put two fingers inside your vagina feeling which way it goes. You will find that your fingers go towards the small of your back at an angle, not straight up the middle of your body. This is the direction at which to point a tampon. You will feel the walls of your vagina hug your fingers; these muscles will also keep the tampon in place. The walls of your vagina will be wet or dry according to what stage you are in your menstrual cycle. The wetness is a natural secretion which lubricates your vagina and keeps it healthy.

If you make a mistake inserting a tampon and lose the cord, don't panic. Tampons cannot get 'lost' in the vagina and cannot pass through the cervix into the womb. Squat down and insert your fingers into your vagina; you should be able to retrieve the tampon. If you really can't get it out, your doctor will fish it out for you.

Bathing

It's perfectly OK to have a bath and wash your hair when you have your period. In fact whether you have a bath or not you should wash well between your legs at least once a day. Once menstrual blood comes into contact with the air, it's quite strong-smelling. To avoid getting blood on clean towels after your bath or wash, insert a tampon before drying and/or dab your vulva dry with tissues. Use a fresh pad and change into clean pants if necessary. If you get bloodstains on your pants or sheets, soak them before washing in cold salt water or in a biological washing power.

Period Pains

About a third of girls have period pains (dysmenorrhoea) in their mid-teens. They get cramping sensations before and during the period. It can be accompanied by backache, sweating, feeling dizzy and wanting to be sick. The short-term strategy for dealing with period pains is to take two aspirin tablets and go to bed with a hot-water bottle to hug against your abdomen until you feel better. If your period pains persist, you should see your doctor. S/he will be able to prescribe treatment to help you; perhaps the pill.

Girls and women who have not experienced period pains are sometimes unsympathetic to sufferers; in schools male teachers often are. It's true that some girls pretend to have period pains to get out of games, but if you're feeling bad and you're not believed you should complain about it when you're feeling better – nobody has period pains for fun.

Premenstrual Tension

Some girls and women find that they get bad-tempered, depressed or tense every month for no apparent reason and/or they feel bloated. If this happens to you, note the days when it occurs in the diary where you keep a record of when your periods start and stop. It may be that there's some very good reason for you to feel depressed and it's nothing to do with your menstrual cycle. But if it happens regularly before your period is due then it may be to do with hormone balance changes which are causing a build-up of fluid in your body. When your period starts you may find that you're urinating (peeing) a lot – getting rid of all the extra water! Sometimes just realising what's causing the tension is enough to enable you to handle it; if you feel really bad you should consult your doctor.

BOY INTO MAN: FIRST STAGES OF PUBERTY

The onset of puberty for boys usually occurs between the ages of 10 and 16 and ends between 14 and 18. You will find that:

1. You grow in height. Some people experience surges of growth and find that none of their clothes fit. They suddenly have to get used to being longer and bigger. They're often awkward and clumsy until they adjust. Other people begin to wonder if they'll ever grow taller; they catch up in the end.
2. You grow in weight. You'll be putting on 8-12 pounds a year until you reach your adult weight. This weight gain is normal and does not mean that you are fat. If you think you've a weight problem you should cut down on things like

sweets and chips and exercise more, but consult your doctor before going on any kind of strict diet – it's not always a good idea to diet when you're growing.

3 You're stronger than you used to be.
4 Your scrotum, testicles (balls) and penis have grown.
5 You're having nocturnal emissions (wet dreams). You wake up one morning to find that you've ejaculated – semen has spurted out of your penis. This usually happens after a sexy dream which is why it's called a 'wet dream'. It's perfectly normal.
6 You voice is 'breaking' – sometimes it's deep and sometimes not.
7 You're growing hair under your armpits.
8 Hair grows above your penis and over your testicles (balls). This is called pubic hair.
9 Some boys find that their breast area becomes tender and either one or both 'breasts' enlarge. This can last a year or so but it will eventually disappear.

BOY INTO MAN: LATER STAGES OF PUBERTY

Your body will continue to change gradually over a number of years until you are a fully grown man. You will find that:

1 Your scrotum, testicles and penis increase in size.
2 You often have erections, sometimes when you're not expecting to.
3 Your face begins to be hairy. You think about shaving.

4 You may develop body hair.
5 Your pubic hair increases and grows coarser. It is usually darker than the hair on your head.
6 You tend to get spots.
7 You sweat more and have to be careful about body odour.

The Male Sex Organs

Between your legs you have a fleshy sac called the scrotum which houses your testicles or testes (balls). Each testicle contains millions of tiny seminiferous (semen-producing) tubules from which comes sperm, the male sex cells. At puberty, sperm production begins and it continues, almost always, for the rest of your life. Sperm is stored in a collection of coiled tubes adjacent to your testicles called the epididymis. From the epididymis, sperm travels up into the main body cavity along tubes called the vas deferens (these are the tubes which are cut in vasectomy), past the seminal vesicles. The seminal vesicles secrete a thick yellow fluid necessary for the survival of the sperm. Inside the prostate gland the two vas deferens tubes join and link-up with the urethra on its way down from the bladder. When you get an erection, a valve is activated that prevents urine (pee) from passing through the erect penis. When your penis is limp, the same valve prevents semen from passing through it. The prostate gland secretes prostatic fluid, the major component of semen. During ejaculation, muscles around the prostate and between the legs contract to propel semen along the urethra and out of the penis. Behind the scrotum is the anus. This is the opening to the rectum. It is small, strong and has numerous nerve-endings. It is used to hold in faeces (shit/turds) and to push them out.

The male sex organs

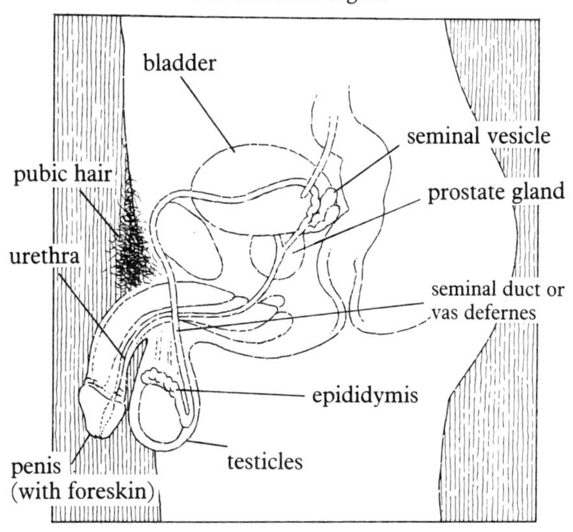

The Penis

The long part of the penis is called the shaft; the tip is called the head or glans. The glans, which is the most sensitive external part of the penis, is covered by a flap of skin called the foreskin. When the penis is erect, the foreskin retracts to reveal the glans. Some boys/men are circumcised – that is, they have had an operation to remove their foreskin. This is done for religious and, sometimes, medical reasons. Having or not having a foreskin makes no difference to sexual feeling. The inside of the penis is made of spongy erectile tissue. When you are sexually excited the erectile tissue fills with blood and the penis stiffens and become erect. Some boys find that their erect penis has a slight bend. This is quite normal and nothing to worry about. Some boys find that one testicle hangs lower than the other or that their testicles are uneven in size. If that's the case with you, that's what's normal for you.

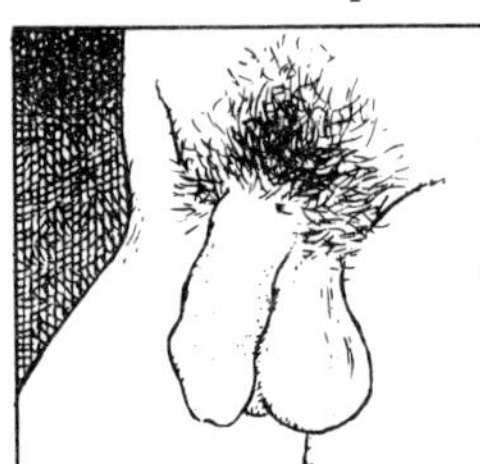
Uncircumcised penis

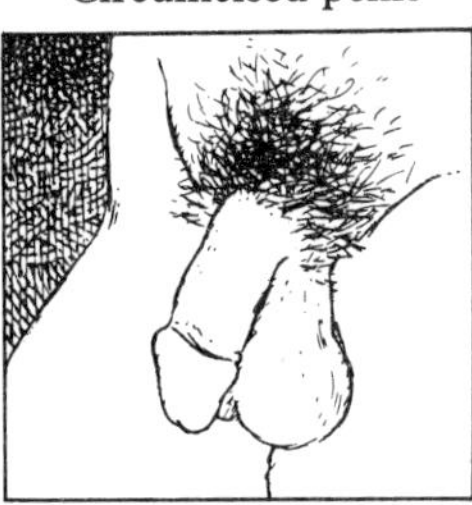
Circumcised penis

Penis Size

In our society a good deal of emphasis is put on penis size despite the fact that most penises are the same – usually 2-3 inches when limp and about 6 inches when erect. Undersized sexual organs are extremely rare. If you genuinely think that yours are, check with your doctor; but before you do so, think about other penises you have seen.

In changing rooms you'll probably have had a glimpse of other people's penises from time to time. Remember that you are looking *across* at theirs and that you look *down* at your own. It could be this difference in perspective that's giving you the idea that your organ is smaller. Don't be fooled either by photographs of erect penises in pornographic magazines – they are carefully photographed from below at angles chosen to make them look gigantic. Experiment with a mirror the next time you have an erection. Hold it below the erection so that you look up at it. You'll find it looks much larger than it does when you look down at it from above. You may see advertisements in sex shops and sex magazines for penis enlargers. These gadgets and creams do not work and they could be dangerous. Don't try them.

You'll find that your scrotum and penis will 'hang' particularly well after a warm bath. This is because they are affected by temperature. The warmer it is, the looser it all hangs; the colder it is (or if you are exercising hard) the more it all hugs your body for warmth and *appears* smaller. If you're feeling relaxed and happy, you'll also find that you 'hang' well.

The important thing to remember is that a lover (who is unlikely to have seen you undressed before agreeing to have sex with you) will choose you because they like *you* – your personality, your overall attractiveness, your sensuality, your tenderness. They won't even have thought about the size of your cock.

Unexpected Erections

Apart from wet dreams, it is quite common for boys to find that they begin to have frequent erections – and not always when they want to (eg during a maths test, on the bus). This is quite normal. Remember that unless you're actually naked other people are not likely to notice. Put your hands in your pockets and think about something very unsexy to help it to go away – which it will in a few minutes. In crowded trains and buses there are sometimes people who like to take the opportunity to grope or rub against other people 'by accident'. Some boys find to their horror that they get an erection, especially if the groper has touched their genitals. This is a mechanical response to the touching and it does not mean that you led the toucher on or that you 'really' wanted it to happen.

Testicular Cancer: Examining your Balls

Cancer of the testicles is quite rare, accounting for only 1% of all cancers in men, but it occurs most commonly in men under 35. Early detection of testicular cancer is very important – that's why you should regularly examine your balls for lumps or unusual swellings. The best time to do this is after a hot bath when the scrotum is relaxed. Place the index and middle fingers of your hands under your testicles and your thumbs on top. Roll each testicle between your thumbs and fingers. They should feel firm but not hard. Also feel for the epididymis, the sperm storage tube behind each testicle. They should feel a bit spongier. If you feel a small hard lump or an unusual thickening or swelling or if you experience discomfort, consult your doctor *at once*. It may be nothing, but if it is cancer, it will need immediate treatment.

It's also a good idea to get into the habit of soaping your balls in the bath or shower with your hands, rather than with a flannel or sponge. That way you're more likely to notice any unusual change in their feel.

HOW A BABY IS CONCEIVED

For a girl/woman to become pregnant, a ripe egg-cell (ovum) in her fallopian tubes must be fertilised by a sperm cell. When a couple have sexual intercourse the man places his erect penis into the woman's vagina. When he ejaculates, the millions of sperm in his semen swim up the vagina into the womb and into the fallopian tubes. If there is a ripe egg cell there a sperm enters it and fertilises it.

It is possible, but rare, for a girl to become pregnant during mutual masturbation if the boy ejaculates near her vulva. (For information on Contraception see p 77.)

If a woman cannot become pregnant because her partner is infertile (he cannot produce sperm), she can be artificially inseminated by a doctor with sperm from a donor. Lesbian women who want to be mothers sometimes become pregnant using this method.

Once fertilised, the egg travels down the fallopian tube, attaches itself to the wall of the womb and its cells begin to divide and grow. The foetus, as the growing baby is now called, is fed from the mother's body through the placenta, a pad of soft tissue through which oxygen passes from the mother's blood to the baby's. A cord, the umbilical cord, grows from the placenta to the middle of the foetus. The lining of the womb becomes a bag filled with fluid in which the foetus floats, protected from knocks or bangs. At the end of about 9 months the baby is ready to be born.

Birth

During the last month of the pregnancy, the baby moves into the position in which it will be born. This is usually head downwards. When it is ready to be born, the muscles of the mother's womb contract and push the baby down through the opening of the womb. The bag which held the baby breaks and the fluid passes out of the body through the vagina. The baby moves through the vagina, which stretches to make room. Finally the baby is pushed out of the vagina and out between the mother's legs. This process is called labour; it usually takes about 7 hours, but second or third babies often arrive more quickly. It is painful and tiring but there is the reward of a baby at the end of it.

After the baby is born the placenta (now called the afterbirth) is expelled. The umbilical cord is cut, leaving a 'belly button' at the place to which it was attached.

PERSONAL HYGIENE

Smells: Nice and Nasty

Once puberty has started, apocrine sweat glands begin to work in your armpits and groin. They produce a pleasant, musky body smell – an adult scent which signals that you are becoming a sexually mature person. This is a nice smell when fresh, but not nice when it gets stale. Puberty is also a time when feeling uneasy or insecure can produce nervous sweating. Add to this the fact that your sebaceous glands (which produce an oily fluid called sebum) get very active at puberty and can cause dead skin cells to clog on your greasy skin.

All this means that good personal hygiene matters a lot during puberty. To keep your body odour attractive and fresh you should aim to wash all over every day if you can, and especially after sports and in hot weather. If you can't have a bath or shower every day, at least be sure to wash your face, your armpits, your genital area and your feet. Always wipe your bottom from front to back to help stop germs from spreading. Remember to wash your neck and ears regularly and clean your nails. You should brush your teeth at least twice a day; after every meal if you can.

If you use a deodorant, remember to wash first and dry thoroughly before you use it. Don't put deodorant on a dirty skin. Girls should never use a vaginal deodorant – they are dangerous and can cause infections.

Boys should take special care to wash their penis properly every day. Under the foreskin are tiny glands which produce a whitish secretion called smegma (it helps the foreskin slide back smoothly). If the smegma is not regularly washed away it will collect, become smelly and may eventually cause a sore red patch to develop on the glans called balanitis. If this happens to you, pull your foreskin right back and clean the area gently with damp cotton wool. Dab it dry. If the infection has not cleared up in a few days go to the doctor. A clean healthy penis is particularly important if you are, or are hoping to be, sexually active. An unclean penis, whether circumcised or not, can increase the possibility of your partner catching an infection; girls' chances of developing cervical cancer increase if their partner has an unclean penis.

Whether you are a girl or a boy, if you are sexually active with a partner, keeping your body, and particularly your genital area, fresh and clean not only makes you more sexually attractive, it's an important part of sexual good manners.

Clean Clothes for Clean Bodies

There's not much point in putting dirty clothes back on after your daily bath/shower/wash. If you haven't got lots of changes of clothes, you're going to have to organise yourself so that what you have got is always washed, dried and ironed for when you need it. Get into the habit of putting on clean underwear and clean socks or tights every day. Girls should ensure that their pants are cotton or have a cotton gusset. This is because cotton is porous; synthetic fibres next to the vulva retain moisture and heat and can help harmful bacteria to grow. Remember that smoking, apart from giving you lung cancer and heart disease, will make your breath and clothes stink.

SPOTS, BLACKHEADS AND ACNE

At puberty it is almost inevitable that your skin will erupt with spots, blackheads and, perhaps, acne. This is because your sebaceous glands have increased in size and number so your skin is greasier, new sweat glands have appeared so your skin is sweatier and the layer of dead cells on the skin (quite normal, everyone has it) increases.

Spots are caused when dirt and germs are caught in the greasy sheen on your skin and cause infection. Blackheads are hardened plugs of sebum trapped under the layer of dead cells. Acne (red or purple lumps) is caused when the sebaceous glands are infected by germs. Unfortunately new glands take a long time to settle down so the only way to deal with skin problems is to get into a good skin-care routine.

What to do

Wash your face thoroughly at least twice a day with warm water and soap. If there are particularly greasy areas (eg your chin, around your nose), massage the lather very thoroughly over these bits. Rinse well with cold water, removing all traces of soap. Towel thoroughly as you dry – the rubbing action will help remove dead skins cells and unlock sebum. If you have non-spotty areas where the skin now feels tight and slightly uncomfortable, rub in some moisturiser.

Sunshine is a great help to some spotty skins because the ultra-violet helps to clear them up. There are lots of lotions and creams available but if you're following the washing routine described above they aren't necessary. If you have really bad acne you should go to your doctor, who may prescribe antibiotics. If, despite all your best efforts, you still have bad spots, then it's just bad luck. Comfort yourself with the thought that most skins settle down by the time you're seventeen.

During the day you can disguise spots with a make-up stick called an eraser (available from chemists).

Squeezing and Picking

Only squeeze spots if they have reached the stage where the pus (it's a yellowish liquid) has gathered at the head of the spot and is pressing against the skin. Pus can be infectious so if you pick carelessly at spots and don't keep washing your hands, you'll spread infection and you might cause scarring. Squeeze blackheads out gently. If they won't budge, leave them.

If you're a boy, wet shaving can increase spottiness or cause a rash. An electric razor may be the answer – perhaps you could have a go with a friend's to see if it suits you. If shaving rashes persist, consult your doctor.

Hair

Head Hair

During puberty your hair may become greasy quite quickly, and look lank and unattractive. The answer is to wash it more frequently using a mild shampoo. Rinse with clear water. If your hair is fine or if you get split ends, use a conditioner.

Face Hair and Body Hair: Girls

During puberty you may get dark hair on your upper lip and the odd hair on your chin. If you're happy about it, that's fine. A shadow of hair on the upper lip can often look attractive. Some girls and women object to our society's view that women shouldn't be hairy, seeing it as another kind of sex stereotyping. They choose not to remove facial hair (or shave their legs etc) for this reason.

If you're not happy about facial hair, there are ways that it can be disguised or removed but it's important to choose the right ways. Do not remove hair on the chin or upper lip by plucking, shaving or using depilatory (hair-removing) creams. If you do shave or cream, you will remove all the hairs on the skin, including very fine down hairs that are not a problem. These fine hairs will then grow back stubbly and your problem will look worse. If you pluck the hairs out, you risk damaging the root. The hairs will grow back thicker and more quickly.

The best way to remove unwanted facial hair on your chin and lip is electrolysis. A fine needle is inserted into the hair follicle by a trained beautician and a small electric current travels down the needle and destroys the hair root. Unfortunately this treatment is expensive *and* it takes a long time. Hairs have to be treated many times in this way before the roots are permanently destroyed and the hairs cannot then grow back. However, once you've had three or four treatments you will find the hairs grow back less quickly and there can be longer periods in between treatments. Electrolysis is available in beauty salons in large department stores. Do not be tempted to send for a mail order electrolysis needle and try to do it yourself, or to have treatment from an unqualified beautician. If you do, you risk permanent scarring. Always ensure that the beautician uses a fresh needle when you have treatments (see p 52 on AIDS).

Electrolysis is also a good way to remove permanently any odd hairs that have grown round your nipples or down from your belly button, if you're unhappy about them.

If you skin is white, a good, if laborious, way to cope with unwanted facial hair is to bleach it. You can buy a special facial hair bleaching pack from large chemist.

You don't have to remove hair from your armpits unless you want to. Lots of girls/women don't; in Spain, Italy, Germany and many other countries hairy female armpits are the norm. You don't have to remove hair from your legs either; again, lots of girls/women don't. Some girls/ women have pubic hair that grows down at the top of their thighs; it's up to you whether you remove it.

The simplest and cheapest way to remove 'bikini line', leg or armpit hair is to shave it. Don't use anyone else's wet-shave razor and don't lend yours. (See p 52 on AIDS). If you're going on holiday and plan to spend a lot of time on the beach, waxing is a good if expensive idea because it lasts longer – the hairs are pulled out by the roots. You can have it done at a beauty salon or buy waxing strips at larger chemists.

Face Hair and Body Hair: Boys

How strong your beard growth will be and when it will start depend on your genetic make-up. Some boys have hairy faces from the age of 13, some boys have no facial hair at 18. Growth does not always follow the same pattern; some boys/men have hairless patches at the sides of their cheeks, some boys/men have hairy growth from the top of their cheek bones all the way down their necks to meet their chest hair. Full beard growth does not establish itself until you're in your twenties.

Once you've started shaving you'll have to go on because cutting the hairs gives you a bristly growth. Not many boys/men look good with 'designer stubble'. If you shave with a wet-shave razor it will take a bit of practice to learn how to shave your particular hair growth. Remember, do not borrow or share wet-shave razors (see p 52 on AIDS).

Some boys/men have hairy arms, fingers, legs, toes, chests and backs and some boys/men have hardly any body hair. If you look at the adult males in your biological family, you'll get an idea of how hairy you're likely to be. Being hairy, or not being hairy, has nothing to do with how sexy you are.

EXERCISE

During puberty lots of people drop out of games and PE at school. Often it's because the choices aren't interesting or you don't like the way it's taught, or it's not seen as a 'cool' thing to do. But if you're not exercising at school, you should be organising some kind of regular exercise for yourself out of school (weight-lifting, keep-fit, swimming, ice-skating, whatever).

Exercise is important for your health, your beauty and for your safety (you should know how strong and how fit you are in case you're ever in a dangerous situation). Exercise is especially important for bodies that are growing and changing. Some people experience growth spurts and can grow four inches in as many months; it's not surprising if they are then clumsy and self-conscious. Sport and exercise help you to adjust to these changes in your size and shape and improve your balance and co-ordination. You'll find that you'll be learning to move confidently and gracefully again without realising it.

Section 2
Sex and Feelings

You and Your Parents/Guardians

During puberty your life is changed not just by the fact that your body is changing and developing but because your emotions and feelings are changing too; your position in society is also different.

To take society first: in some parts of the world you would already be considered an adult or almost an adult because in such societies adult status is dependent on physical development. A girl will become a woman, for example, following her first period. In our technologically advanced society, physically mature or almost physically mature young people are not considered adults. Your education and training will continue at least until the age of 16 and perhaps beyond, and there are many areas of 'adult' life that you will not be able to enter for several years. This puts young people into a difficult limbo-land – physically adults or nearly adults and yet dependent on parents/guardians for food, shelter and money and to a large extent denied responsibility and autonomy.

As you move on into puberty you will be growing spiritually, emotionally and intellectually as well as physically. You will be confronting for yourself things that you used to accept without question or take at face value, and be actively working out where you stand. You will also be filled with intense sexual feelings and preoccupations that make you swing from being introvert and dreamy to being extrovert and sociable. Parents/guardians and others often find it hard to accept that you're breaking away from them and forming your own values and views of the world. And, although they probably wouldn't admit it, they may also find it hard to accept that you're now a person with sexual feelings and desires.

Some parents/guardians feel hurt and upset that their baby (that's you) who used to listen to them with trust and wonder and who used to depend on them, no longer seems to need them. They sometimes express this hurt by making a silly fuss over things that symbolise you-the-new-adult. They may say, for example, that their daughter is not ready to wear a bra or their son has no need to shave, despite obvious evidence to the contrary. Not all parents/guardians are like this of course. If yours are, try to reassure them that having a teenage daughter/son doesn't mean an end to loving and caring – from them to you and from you to them. It should be possible to work out a new deal about the ways that you all get on together – one that acknowledges that you are a young adult, able to be a responsible person. If things are really impossible, with tension and rows all the time, you should contact the organisations listed under *Counselling* at the back of this book for advice.

Becoming a Sexual Person

You are your body and as you go on into puberty you'll find that you become preoccupied with sex and filled with intense sexual feelings. This is quite normal and very nice – in fact it would be a bit odd if all your newly-developed adult sexual equipment *didn't* produce sexual feelings and desires.

The expression of your sexual feelings will be very much a matter of the particular relationship you are in, and of your preferences and needs in relation to your partner's preferences and needs. You can't be a sexual person in isolation, and part of caring about and respecting the rest of the human race is understanding and respecting their sexual feelings, which may not be the same as yours. Gaining such knowledge about others should be part of your sex education. Even if you feel that bits of this book don't apply to you ('I'm gay, why should I read about heterosexuals?'; 'I'm a boy, why should I read about periods?'), I hope you'll be interested enough in other people to want to read them.

The expression of our sexual feelings and needs can't be isolated from the rest of our lives. Sexual feelings and sexual activities are expressions of our desire/love/infatuation/trust/passion for another being and cannot be taken out of the context of our responsibilities for that person. Sex and sexual feelings are not just about techniques and methods – they are about your whole body, your identity, your values, the way you interact with other people, how you value yourself and how you value others.

Sexual Violence and Unwanted Sexual Attention

You and you alone have the right to control what happens to your body. No one should be allowed to:

- make you feel uncomfortable or embarrassed about your body
- touch you if you don't want to be touched

- coerce or bribe you into sexual activity that you are not sure about or don't want
- assault you for their sexual enjoyment
- misuse their authority to impose on you sexually.

And you, of course, do not have the right to do any of these things to other people.

At some point in their life almost everyone suffers some form of unwanted sexual attention – perhaps you get an obscene phonecall, or a man exposes himself to you, or your date tries to force you to go further than you want to. Sometimes people are sexually assaulted, raped or become victims of incest. Young people are particularly vulnerable to sexual attack – 70% of the victims of reported rape are under 25, for example. This is because you are attractive, with a sexually mature or almost sexually mature body and are at a point in your life when you are going out more and experimenting with new situations and people. It's important to take commonsense precautions to keep yourself safe while developing your independence. I discuss this in detail in my book *Too Close Encounters and What to do About Them* (Piccadilly/Magnet).

Some kinds of strange sexual behaviour are dangerous and others are not. You should know about them so that you can recognise them and take the appropriate self-preservation action if you need to.

Flashers

Flashers are people (almost always men) who expose their genitals in public. It's thought that they like to shock people and then fantasise around the incident afterwards. Ninety-five per cent of male flashers expose with a limp penis (ie they don't have an erection that makes their penis stick out) and they are not thought to be dangerous.

They will not go on to attack you. Five per cent of male flashers do expose with an erect penis and they could go on to attack you. If you are confronted with one of this tiny minority, try to run away or get help. Flashers should be reported to the police.

Obscene Phonecallers

Obscene phonecallers (almost always men) are thought to be sexual inadequates who masturbate as they make their calls. They are not thought to be dangerous – they will not go on to attack you. But these calls can be very frightening and disturbing. Get a man to answer the phone; if the calls don't stop, get your number changed and report the incidents to the police.

Rubbers and Touchers (frotteurs)

These people (usually men) like to take advantage of crowded trains or shops to rub against you or touch you. Move away if you can and shout out loudly, eg 'Keep your filthy hands to yourself!'

Peeping Toms (voyeurs)

Peeping Toms (usually men) like to spy on people undressing, naked or making love: they are not thought to go on to attack people. Take common-sense precautions so you're not overlooked in your private and intimate moments. Report peeping Toms to the police.

Sexual Assault and Rape

Rapists and sexual assailants can be weird strangers who jump out at you and grab you, but they can also be people you know and would assume to be 'normal' and trustworthy. Sixty per cent of reported rapes are committed by someone known to the victim. Take sensible precautions to keep yourself safe in the street, and keep your home secure. Form relationships where the overall balance of power in terms of age, experience and money is about equal so that you will not be intimidated or pressurised into sexual activity that you don't want. Be realistic about the fact that people who seem to be nice can turn out to have sex-typed notions about female/male sexual behaviour – it's still not uncommon, for example, for a boy to assume that a girl who agrees to come up to his flat for coffee is actually agreeing to sex. There is a subtle but crucial difference between persuading and *forcing* and between cajoling and *coercing* someone into sexual activity that some people do not grasp. In this book I list *Sexual Good Manners,* ways of not hurting or exploiting others sexually, and I also list examples of exploitative sexual behaviour which you should avoid for yourself and learn to spot in others.

WHEN SHOULD YOU HAVE SEX?

There is no 'should' about having sex at all. Some people aren't interested in sex and live very happy lives without it. Others are interested. If you're one of them you will, at your own pace, become sexually ready and want to have sexual experiences. There are legal restrictions concerning the age at which you can have sex; these are explained on p 96 of this book.

It's important to realise that the expression of tenderness, love and affection need not necessarily or need not always be sexual. Sex is often presented to us as a series of steps that starts with kissing and leads inexorably to sexual intercourse. But one step does not have to lead to another, unless you both want it to. Sometimes what is wanted is an expression of affection – being hugged or cuddled or kissed. There are many ways to express physical closeness, intimacy, affection and love, and sexual intercourse is only one of them.

SEXUAL GOOD MANNERS

Everyone deserves to be well treated and not to have their self-esteem hurt. Sometimes you don't realise that you are hurting the other person, or you feel poorly treated and you're not sure why. What are needed very often are simply good sexual manners; by this I mean behaviour that respects other people's sexual rights and does not set out to exploit or demean them.

1. Do not assume that your girl/boyfriend is exactly like you, with precisely the same needs and feelings. Take time to get to know her/him and learn to respond to her/his feelings and needs. It's called sharing and it's a lovely thing to do.
2. You don't have to have sex to have a good relationship with your girl/boyfriend.
3. Do not pressurise your girl/boyfriend into sexual activity by making her/him feel bad ('You don't love me enough') or by threatening her/him ('There's plenty of other girls/boys I can go out with if you won't do it').
4. You do not have to have sex to prove you love your girl/boyfriend. If it doesn't feel comfortable and good to go ahead with sexual activity, then don't.
5. Do not take advantage of your girl/boyfriend's ignorance about sex to push her/him into going further than s/he really wants to.

6 Do not take sexual advantage of your girl/boyfriend if s/he is too drunk or too high to know what's going on.
7 Do not reveal intimate details about your girl/boyfriend to the world. It's cruel and shows that you are untrustworthy. Sexual activity is private.
8 Do not expect sexual favours in return for spending money on someone (eg taking them out to dinner).
9 If you know that your girl/boyfriend has slept with someone before, do not assume that they must therefore sleep with you. What happened before is none of your business.
10 If you have slept with someone once, that doesn't mean that you're obliged to keep on sleeping with that person, or obliged to sleep with anyone else if you don't want to. Saying yes once doesn't commit you to always saying yes.
11 If you're genuinely not sure whether your girl/boyfriend means what they say when they say no to sexual activity, then you can ask again in a different way. Say, for example, 'I know people sometimes think they have to say no to sex when they really want to say yes. Is that what you're doing now?' If the answer is still no, then accept it and don't try to pressurise your girl/boyfriend to change their mind.
12 Just because someone's attracted to you doesn't mean that you are in any way sexually obliged to them. Say no.

(Adapted from *Too Close Encounters and What to do About Them* by Rosemary Stones)

Exploitative Sexual Behaviour

There are ways of behaving that are not just uncaring but which exploit other people. Perhaps we've all done one or two of these nasty things in our worse moments but watch out for someone who:

1. is extremely self-centred and not interested in other people's needs and feelings
2. gets angry or sulky when they don't get their own way
3. manipulates people to get their own way using emotional pressure or bribery
4. is convinced that they have a right to always get what they want
5. exploits other people's sense of decency and trust
6. makes sexual jokes which reveal a contemptuous attitude towards sexual partners or girl/boyfriends
7. treats their girl/boyfriends as a sex object rather than as a person
8. is excessively jealous and possessive, always supposing that their girl/boyfriend fancies someone else
9. belittles their girl/boyfriend in public by ignoring them or flirting with someone else
10. has sexual relationships with girls/boys from a different social class or different ethnic group because they think that class/group is inferior, and when they would not dream of having a sexual relationship with someone from their own class/group.
11. has sexual relationships with girls/boys from a different social class or ethnic group in order to 'avenge' themself on that class/group.

(Adapted from *Too Close Encounters and What to do About Them* by Rosemary Stones)

Some people believe, for religious cultural or moral reasons, that sex should only take place within marriage. If that's your view, that's fine; as I've already said, sex cannot be isolated from the rest of your life and from your values. You should, though, be aware of the danger of confusing very strong sexual desire with love. If you know, in your heart of hearts, that you're really planning to get married because you're dying to have sex, then it's time for some serious re-thinking.

Some people have sex because all their friends do. This may sound ridiculous but in fact peer-group pressure is a major reason for many young people to start sexual activity. It's the 'norm' in the group they move in and they're afraid to be different in case they're rejected.

Peer-group pressure often affects girls and boys differently. Boys are often expected to be sexually active even when they're not and don't want to be. Sometimes they have to pretend to have 'scored' because if they don't play the macho-stud game, they're seen as 'wimps'. Girls are often put in a no-win situation – if they do have sex they're seen as 'slags' and fair game for any boy; if they don't they're seen as 'tight bitches'. This kind of pressure can also push young people into couple relationships earlier than they would have wanted, and makes it hard for them to explore their feelings at their own pace.

Within this scenario, the fact that at least one in ten young people is gay remains unacknowledged. Their sexuality is not recognised, and if being gay is referred to at all, it's invariably in a crude, dismissive and bigoted way.

This depressing picture is, thankfully, no longer as universal as it was. These days, there are young people who are breaking away from sex-typed expectations of female and male behaviour and who accept that different people come to sexual activity at a different pace, when they are ready and the circumstances are right. You should not feel forced to have intercourse just because your partner is aroused. Neither, of course, should you put pressure on your partner if you are aroused but s/he does not feel ready. People, boys as well as girls, can control themselves. Wait until if feels comfortable and right for both of you. First sexual experiences are important because they can affect your sex life for a long time afterwards.

Some people want to wait until they meet someone very special. Some people like to experiment sexually; that's fine as long as the people you're experimenting with feel the same way about it and you're all taking responsibility for safer sex and for contraception. Do not mislead or exploit other people's feelings.

Sexual relationships do end for all kinds of reasons and people eventually start new ones. People do not always meet the 'right person' for them easily; some people do not believe that there is one 'right person'. If you've slept with someone it doesn't mean that you're tied to her/him for life. Bonds are created by sex but don't allow yourself to feel trapped by what may have been a mistake. Remember, you have the rest of your life to live.

Some people feel terribly sexually unattractive (perhaps they have a bad case of acne or puppy fat or no nice clothes to wear) and they're sure no one will ever fancy them. Some people feel like a fish out of water because they don't get to meet other people who share their interests or outlook on life. Remember that acne and puppy fat gradually disappear; you may be able to solve the clothes problem by ingenuity or a Saturday job and, as you get older, you'll be able to move around more and meet new people who are more your cup of tea. As I've said, it's not always easy to meet the 'right person' for you.

Sexual Dreams and Fantasies

Part of becoming a mature sexual person is having dreams and fantasies about sex. This is quite normal.

You may find that you dream or fantasise about people you know, although in real life you wouldn't have any kind of sexual relationship with them. You may find that your dreams/fantasies involve rape or being raped, sex with some glamorous stranger, sex with more than one person. You may even dream/fantasise about sex with your own relatives, your parents, sisters or brothers.

All this is quite common. There is no sexual dream or fantasy that you have that lots of other people have not also had. What you should remember is that you control your day-dreams and fantasies and can change them or end them if they make you feel uncomfortable. Such dreams/fantasies do not mean that in real life you want to be raped or commit incest or any of the other things you might fantasise or dream about. Dreams/fantasies are often about forbidden or taboo behaviour and situations, which you would not enact in real life. Fantasies about rape are common because lots of people feel guilty about their sexual feelings and like to imagine a situation in which moral responsibility is taken away from them.

If you have such dreams/fantasies and you are then the victim of a sexual assault or incest in real life, do not imagine that you are therefore to blame, that you 'really' wanted it to happen. There is no automatic connection between your sexual dreams/fantasies and real-life sexual violence.

SECTION 3
SEX AND SOCIETY

ATTITUDES TO SEX

Today single women choose, without stigma, to bring up their children alone; pop stars, politicians and others talk openly about being lesbian or gay; people do not feel constrained to live out lives of misery in marriages that have failed; unmarried people and teenagers can seek confidential advice about contraception from their doctors and women may legally seek termination of an unwanted pregnancy rather than resort to dangerous illegal abortions. (Not all of this is the case in the Republic of Ireland.)

These things have not come about by magic, but by years of brave campaigning by social reformers; in recent years the tenacity and determination of groups from the Women's Movement have been particularly important. The now often sneered-at 'permissive sixties' was in fact a liberating and influential period – a generation of young people joined together to reject many of the stigmatising and stifling values of the 'traditional' family and celebrate peace and love. That there can, with hindsight, be many criticisms of that time, does not detract from its tremendous impact on attitudes today to sex and to sexual freedom.

It's important that your generation of young adults realise that in the past those who did not fit into the 'traditional' family – unmarried mothers and their illegitimate children, divorced people, homosexuals and lesbians – suffered and were punished by being found socially unacceptable or by being denied employment opportunities. Even today, members of the British Secret Service who are revealed to be homosexual are assumed to be a security risk. In her autobiography *Our Kate*, best-selling novelist Catherine Cookson describes vividly how, as an illegitimate child, she was insulted by adults and children and not invited to other children's parties: "You have no da!" It was not until she was in her fifties that Catherine Cookson found the courage to say publicly that she is illegitimate.

This is not in any way to dismiss marriage and the family; a great many people find happiness and fulfilment within them and will continue to do so. It's important to recognise, though, that 'family' can also mean single-parent families and that there are many other relationships and groups within which people find happiness.

With the advent of AIDS there has been renewed talk about 'sexual permissiveness' and a call for a return to the values of the 'traditional family'. This is actually an attempt to frighten people into being sexually faithful to one partner by suggesting that they will otherwise die of AIDS. Of course some people are, and want to be, sexually faithful to one person, but some don't. It's simply unrealistic to try and make people change their sexual behaviour by threatening them with death. In the days before penicillin when people died of syphilis, they didn't all decide to remain faithful to one partner. Ibsen's play *Ghosts* (1881) is about hypocrisy in a most respectable 'traditional family' in which a man infects his wife with syphilis, thereby passing it on to his son.

People do not easily change their sexual behaviour

despite their best intentions. Often all that happens is that they are less honest about it. This will increase rather than halt the spread of AIDS. What is really needed is the open and positive promotion of sex education and of information about AIDS and about how to practise safer sex so that every young person can apply that knowledge to the way they live their life.

STRAIGHT, GAY, BI AND OTHER LABELS

Some human beings are only sexually attracted to members of the opposite sex. They are called heterosexuals or described as 'straight'. Some human beings are only sexually attracted to members of the same sex. They are called homosexuals or gays. Many female homosexuals prefer to be called lesbians. Some human beings are sexually attracted to members of the opposite sex *and* members of the same sex. they are called bisexuals.

These labels ('gay', 'straight', 'lesbian' etc) are not always very useful, though. People sometimes call themselves one of the labels ('I'm a lesbian woman'; 'I'm straight'; 'I'm a gay man'), but their actual sexual behaviour does not always fit the label. For example, a man who says he is heterosexual may occasionally have sex with other men; a woman who says she's a lesbian may sometimes sleep with a man.

This happens not because people are dreadful liars, but because human sexual behaviour is endlessly variable and labels are inadequate. Labels can be effective for political purposes – the annual Gay Pride March in London, for example, usefully draws attention to continuing legal and other discriminations against gay people. Undoubtedly many of the marchers who define themselves as gay will never have had a sexual relationship with someone from the opposite sex; but some will. Among the onlookers there will be heterosexual people who have never had a sexual relationship with someone from the same sex; but some will. It's important that you understand this, not just because it's interesting to know about human sexual behaviour (which is surprisingly under-researched), but because it matters if you are to practise safer sex and protect yourself against HIV infection/AIDS. An important part of practising safer sex is being cautious about accepting the labels people give themselves and realising that they may in fact practise high-risk sexual behaviour. (AIDS is explained from p 52 onwards in this book.)

Defining Your Sexuality

Are you heterosexual, homosexual, lesbian or bisexual? Actually you don't have to decide right now, or at all if you don't want to. As I've said, labels aren't always very useful. The majority of the population are heterosexual (straight); it's thought that one person in ten is homosexual (gay) or lesbian; no one seems to know how many people are bisexual. Today gay people are still discriminated against but things are better than they used to be. This is largely due to the efforts of social reformers in the 1960s and to the gay community itself, in particular the Campaign for Homosexual Equality (CHE).

Some people say that they knew from early childhood that they were straight or that they were gay. Others don't get a clear idea until much later. Because gay and lesbian people are still discriminated against, many young people who are gay or lesbian deny it to themselves and to the outside world. If this is happening to you it can be very lonely and distressing. At the back of this book I list organisations who will listen sympathetically and be glad to counsel and support you. If you are worried about how your parents/guardians will react if they learn that you are gay, these organisations are experienced at helping young people to deal with that.

People in their early teens often get 'crushes' at school. The objects of these affections don't necessarily indicate whether you will be straight or gay. It's quite common, for example, for a girl who later turns out to be straight to have a crush on another girl or on a woman teacher.

SECTION 4
AIDS AND SAFER SEX

Deciding to have sex has never been easy. When you're ready, willing and eager, perhaps the person you fancy isn't or perhaps you have nowhere private to go. If you are heterosexual, contraception must be thought about *before* you have sex. Whether you are heterosexual or homosexual there is the problem of sexually transmitted diseases and, most seriously of all, there is now the problem of AIDS.

WHAT IS AIDS?

AIDS stands for Acquired Immune Deficiency Syndrome and it is usually a fatal disease. It can affect females and males, heterosexual and gay people and it is something that we all have to learn about and understand. AIDS is caused by a virus, Human Immunodeficiency Virus, or HIV. The virus attacks the body's immune system which is designed to ward off disease. When the body is infected by HIV the immune system is damaged and the body cannot then protect itself from infections and cancers. It is these cancers and infections which cause death.

At the time of writing, despite scientists' best efforts, no antidote or cure has been found for AIDS, although certain treatments are now available. People who catch HIV may develop AIDS and then die. If you are sexually active or are planning to be sexually active *you must learn about AIDS and about how to protect yourself from it by practising Safer Sex.*

How You Don't Catch AIDS

There are lots of myths and misunderstandings around about the way AIDS is transmitted. You cannot get AIDS from:

- touching an infected person. The Princess of Wales has shaken hands with many people with AIDS; the Pope has embraced people with AIDS.
- sharing things like bus seats, door-knobs, phones, towels, soap, swimming-pools, library books, make-up, clothes, lavatory seats, showers, plates, knives and forks, mugs, food, etc.
- hugging, kissing in a social or family way, holding hands, being sneezed on or breathed on, dancing, wrestling, massage, etc.

How You Do Catch AIDS

The virus which causes AIDS, HIV, was discovered as recently as 1983 so it's not surprising that scientists still don't know everything about how it is transmitted, let alone how to cure it. Discoveries about the disease are being made all the time. From the way that it has spread so far, it is however quite certain that AIDS can be caught by vaginal or anal sex with an infected person (see p 71 on sexual intercourse). These are *high-risk activities*. There are also sexual activities which are considered to be *medium-risk* or *low-risk*. Experts advise that, until and unless there is definite evidence to the contrary, you should practise safer sex in relation to these too. From now on in this book, whenever sexual activity is described it is given a *high-risk, medium-risk, low-risk* or *no-risk* rating.

High-Risk Activities

You can become infected by HIV:

1 if you have vaginal or anal intercourse with an infected person. HIV can be passed on from a boy to a girl, from a boy to a boy and from a girl to a boy. To minimise the risk of catching the virus from an infected person you should always use a condom.
2 if you share needles and syringes for injecting drugs with an infected person. When people inject, some of their blood goes up into the needle and syringe. Often the amount is so small you can't see it, but it's there. If someone with HIV infection/AIDS injects and then lends the used syringe or needle to you, you'll be injecting HIV straight into your bloodstream. *Never* share needles or syringes. If you or your sexual partner have shared a syringe with anyone in the past, you should follow safer sex guidelines and seek advice from the AIDS advisory organisations listed in this book. I also list organisations which help with drug dependency.
3 if you share sex toys with an infected person without first sterilising them. HIV is contained in the genital secretions and blood of an infected person.

Medium-Risk Activities

It is thought possible but unlikely that you can become infected by HIV:

1 if you have oral sex with an infected person
2 if you come into contact with infected blood when receiving cosmetic or fringe medical treatment (eg acupuncture, tattooing, ear-piercing, electrolysis). Always check before such treatments that equipment has been sterilised.

Low-Risk Activities

It is thought possible but very unlikely that you might be infected by HIV:

1 if you French kiss with an infected person, exchanging a large amount of saliva. (French kissing is open-mouth kissing with tongue and teeth contact.) The saliva of an infected person contains minute quantities of HIV. You would need to be in contact with considerable amounts to be infected.
2 if you share a toothbrush or wet-shave razor with an infected person. Brushing the teeth sometimes causes bleeding from the gums; wet shaving may cause nicks to the skin. Do not share or lend toothbrushes or wet-shave razors. If you have a wet shave at a barber's, check first that the razor has been sterilised.

Blood for Medical Purposes

There is now no risk in Britain that people who need blood or blood products for medical reasons (eg haemophiliacs, people undergoing surgery etc) can catch HIV. All such blood and blood products are tested and treated to kill any virus that may be present. (This is not the case in some countries, where medical sterilisation equipment is often inadequate and blood not always screened for HIV.) Before these precautions were introduced in Britain, a number of haemophiliacs (people whose blood does not clot and who require clotting factor) were infected by blood products containing HIV.

HOW CAN YOU TELL IF YOU'VE GOT THE AIDS VIRUS?

The only way to find out if you've been infected by HIV is to have a blood test to see if you are antibody positive. You should wait at least 3 months after any risky sexual activity before going for a test. This is because it can take up to 3 months for the body to develop antibodies to HIV. If you're tested before the antibodies have had time to develop, the result may be a 'false negative'. You may still carry the virus and be able to infect others.

If you're feeling anxious about whether or not you have been infected you should ring an AIDs advisory service or consult your nearest STD clinic about whether or not to have a test. It is not advisable to ask your GP to arrange a test for you; insurance companies (who ask GPs about your state of health before giving policies) are now asking GPs not just whether people are HIV positive or not but whether they have ever asked for a test. If you decide to be tested, have it done at an STD clinic where confidentiality and anonymity will not be infringed.

Whether you are infected or not, you need to practise safer sex of course. If you are infected you have a responsibility to protect other people; if you're not infected you need to protect yourself. Remember if your test is negative this doesn't mean you couldn't be infected in the future – you will need to continue to practise safer sex.

The babies of mothers infected by HIV can contract the disease. If you are pregnant and think you may have been infected, contact your nearest STD clinic or ring an AIDS advisory service for advice about whether to have a test *at once*; do not wait before seeking advice about testing.

For information about HIV testing and the law, see p 106.

How Do You Know if Your Partner Has HIV Infection Or AIDS?

The short answer is, you don't. Even in close, trusting relationships where you would expect people to be frank with each other about their sexual behaviour and previous sexual relationships, casual sexual encounters or affairs are sometimes not revealed because one partner fears hurting or losing the other. Sexual relationships are very much tied up with feelings of security and trust as well as with feelings of love so it's not surprising that great significance is often attached to a partner's fidelity or infidelity.

Although sex is much talked about these days – sex education in schools, television discussion programmes, magazine articles etc – because of its private nature, people are rarely open about their actual sexual behaviour. And as I have said before, human sexual behaviour does not lend itself to labelling. It is sensible, if you are in any doubt or if you simply do not know whether your sexual partner is free from HIV infections/AIDS to:

1 always use a condom as a matter of course
2 take whatever you're told about your partner's sexual history and habits with a large pinch of salt

(unless you're ready to trust her/him with your life)

3 not think of your partner in terms of labels like 'gay', 'straight', 'lesbian' etc. It's safer and more realistic to think in terms of sexual *activity* – yours and your partner's.

If you're in any doubt or if your partner refuses to use a condom, *don't have sex*. What are you doing in bed anyway with someone you can't talk to sensibly about safer sex?

PROTECTING YOURSELF AND YOUR PARTNER AGAINST HIV INFECTION OR AIDS

A condom is the best known protection against AIDS. It is possible to catch HIV from an infected person even if a condom is used, but a condom minimises the risk. A condom is a sheath made of very thin rubber which is fitted onto an erect penis before intercourse. When the boy ejaculates ('comes'), his semen stays within the sheath. If the boy is infected with HIV, his partner is protected. If the partner is infected, the boy wearing the condom is protected.

For extra protection you should use a condom in conjunction with a spermicide containing nonoxynol-9. Further on, I list safe brands of condoms (those which passed a recent Consumers' Association test and/or have the BSI Kitemark) and a list of lubricating spermicides containing nonoxynol-9.

If you are having vaginal sex you will also need to think about contraception. Condoms are a form of contraception, but not reliable enough. If you are a sexually active girl it is sensible to seek contraceptive advice from your doctor who may prescribe the pill *while at the same time* you should insist that your partner uses a condom to protect you from HIV.

Choosing a Condom and Spermicide

Condoms sometimes split or leak so it's important to buy a good-quality product. The condoms listed here are the stronger, more reliable brands. When a condom is used as a contraceptive, doctors recommend using a spermicide in addition to the condom. Some spermicides contain nonoxynol-9 which also gives some protection against HIV infection. It is sensible to use a condom with a spermicide containing nonoxynol-9 or a condom coated with nonoxynol-9 if you don't know or are not sure whether your partner is free from HIV infection. This applies whether you are having vaginal or anal sex.

Condoms coated with nonoxynol-9:

Durex Elite
Durex Gold
Durex Nu-form Extra Safe
Jiffi Gold
Knight Barrier
Prime
Mates Standard
Play Mates
Tough Mates (an extra strong condom, less likely to split during anal intercourse)

Condoms with which you should use a spermicide containing nonoxynol-9:

Aegis Snugfit
Blausiegel Hauch-dunn Extra
Duet Supersafe Fully Shaped
Duet Supersafe Ultra Thin
Gold Night
Lambutt Safetex
Lambutt Tru-shape
Lifestyles Nuda
Lifestyles Stimula
Mentor

Durex Arouser
Durex Black Shadow
Durex Fetherlite
Durex Fiesta
Durex Gossamer
Forget-Me-Not
Red Stripe
HT Special (an extra strong condom, less likely to split during anal intercourse

Lubricating spermicides containing nonoxynol-9:

1. **Pessaries:**
   Double Check
   Orthoforms
   Staycept
   Two's Company
2. **Creams and Jellies:**
   Delfen Cream
   Gynol II
   Ortho-Creme
3. **Foams:**
   Delfen Foam
   Emko Contraceptive Foam

Do not use petroleum jelly or baby oil or any oil-based preparation as a lubricant as these can weaken the rubber of a condom; they also provide no protection against HIV infection.
(These products were either recommended by a recent Consumers' Association test and/or have the British Standards Institute's Kite mark.)

If you are having anal sex you should know that this is the highest-risk form of sex. You must use an extra-strong condom and a lubricating spermicide containing nonoxynol-9.

Condoms are cheap and easy to buy (from chemists, some fashion shops, increasingly from chain stores), or can be obtained free from Family Planning Clinics. You don't need a prescription to buy them. Girls as well as boys should carry condoms if there is any possibility that sex may happen. A condom should be seen as just another accessory, along with your keys, comb, filofax and credit card. Carrying a condom doesn't mean you're going to have sex; it does mean that if you decide to, you're prepared and both you and your partner will be protected from the risk of HIV.

How to Put on a Condom

There's no need to feel shy about using a condom or insisting that one is used. Putting one on together can be an erotic and exciting part of lovemaking. Besides, it's better to feel a bit uncomfortable about a condom than to risk getting AIDS. Of course it's harder for girls to insist on a condom being used since it's the boy who has to wear it. If your partner refuses to wear a condom (or let you wear one), don't let yourself be pressurised into having sex. If they're not willing to use a condom, they're not responsible enough to be having sex. What are you doing with this self-centred creep anyway?

It's very important to put a condom on correctly or you risk tearing it. If you haven't see one before you should buy a packet and experiment with them in private. If you are a girl you can practise putting them on over two fingers or over something like a candle. Throw away these condoms when you've finished experimenting with them. They cannot now be used for the real thing.

When you are having sex, as soon as a boy has an erection and *before* his penis touches his partner's sex organs, the condom should be unwrapped and the tip squeezed to expel any air. The condom should then be unrolled over the full length of the penis. Some condoms have a little teat at the end for semen; if this one doesn't, leave a little spare room at the tip. If the condom is not already coated with a spermicidal lubricant (some brands are, some aren't – see p 59), spread lubricating spermicide cream, jelly or foam on the condom before the penis is inserted. When the boy has ejaculated, his semen is contained at the tip of the condom. Soon after ejaculation the boy should slowly and carefully withdraw his penis, holding the condom firmly in place at the base of the penis.

Remember:

- do not unroll a condom before use
- do not use petroleum jelly, baby oil or any oil-based preparation with a condom as these will weaken the rubber (spermicides, KY jelly and Duragel are fine)
- do not use two condoms for extra protection. In fact the friction between the two layers of rubber would tear the condom.

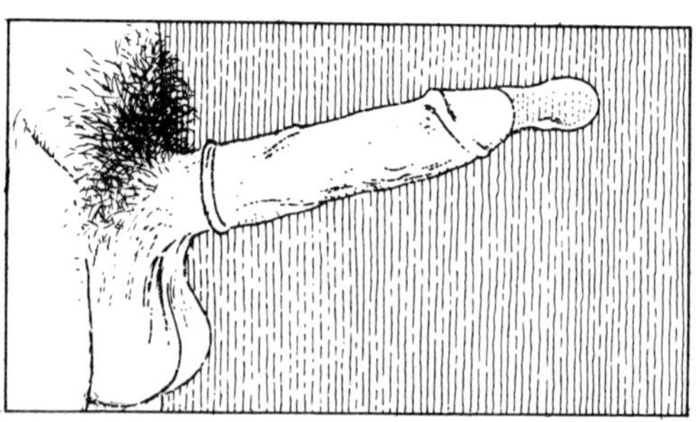

A condom in position over an erect penis, the small teat at the end holds ejaculated semen

At the time of writing there is news of a new condom designed to be used by girls/women (by insertion into the vagina). They are not yet generally available.

WHAT TO DO IF SOMEONE YOU KNOW GETS HIV INFECTION OR AIDS

Finding out that someone you know has HIV infection/AIDS can be a tremendous shock. So far in Britain HIV infection/AIDS has been outside most people's experience. It's not likely to stay that way. Some experts consider that the rate at which the infection is spreading means that in the next couple of years many of us will have the experience of friends or relatives getting HIV infection or AIDS.

Sometimes the shock of discovering that someone has HIV infection or AIDS is made worse by the fact that you did not previously know that that person injected drugs or was gay or bisexual. (At the moment people who inject drugs, gay men (not gay women) and bisexuals are the groups of people most at risk from AIDS in Britain. But the disease is now spreading among heterosexuals in Britain, and particularly among the sexually-active young.)

If you discover that a friend or relative has HIV infection/AIDS, your initial reaction will probably be shock, a feeling of helplessness and great sorrow. It's a good idea to try to think practically about ways that you can care for that person. One very simple but important way is to show her/him that you are not afraid of her/him. As you know, you cannot catch HIV infection or AIDS from touching, hugging or kissing in a social way. Nor can you catch HIV infection or AIDS by sharing things like books, headphones, food and drink.

Someone with HIV infection or AIDS will be feeling profound sorrow, fear, anger and frustration. If you can, show her/him that you are willing to talk about their illness and listen to their feelings. Like anyone else, people with HIV infection or AIDS want friends with whom they can be honest and feel at ease. There are now a number of regional AIDS groups which provide counselling for people with HIV infection/AIDS and their relatives and friends.

SECTION 5
ENJOYING SEX

There is no 'order' to be followed in the way that these sexual activities are listed. Each is valid in its own right. If you're not yet ready for sex, this section explains how it works and what you can look forward to.

HUGGING, HOLDING AND CUDDLING

The warmth and closeness of another's body is a pleasure that we all crave for. Of course you can, and I hope you do, hug and hold in a social and family way with your parents/guardians, your sisters and brothers if you have them, and with your friends. But don't forget that this 'simple' pleasure is also very important with your sexual partner . Standing and holding, sitting and holding, lying and holding – all are pleasurable, comforting, affectionate and loving things to do; hugging and holding with naked bodies can be very exciting and erotic.
AIDS Safety Rating: No Risk

KISSING

The mouth is a very sensual organ. You can kiss lightly with closed mouth or you can French kiss with your

mouth open using your tongue and teeth, tasting each other's saliva. You can kiss your partner's whole body, lick and rub your lips over it.
AIDS Safety Rating: Light kissing and body kissing – No Risk. French kissing – Low Risk

MASTURBATION, FOREPLAY, NON-PENETRATIVE SEX

Non-penetrative sex means that one partner is not penetrated, in the vagina or in the anus, by the other partner. Non-penetrative sex can be a total sexual experience in itself, perhaps resulting in orgasm, or its techniques can be used to precede penetrative sex. When this happens it is called 'foreplay'. Solo masturbation, mutual masturbation and foreplay all involve the same non-penetrative sexual techniques of touching and rubbing the genitals.

Both girls and boys masturbate. It's a natural part of sexual self-exploration, a way of discovering and satisfying your own sexual needs. You'll probably find that you'll masturbate from time to time throughout your sexual life even if you have a sexual partner; your partner may be away or ill or your sex drive may be stronger than your partner's. Enjoy and value solo masturbation as a sexual experience in its own right – it's not second-rate or stop-gap sex; it's just different sex. Mutual masturbation can take place between a girl and a boy, or between two boys or between two girls. It is one of the most common forms of lesbian sex.

Girls masturbate, or can be sexually stimulated by a partner, by rubbing the clitoris directly or indirectly with the hands, or, for example, on the edge of a chair or by spraying water from a shower head over the clitoris. Since the clitoris is not in a rigidly fixed position, any rubbing of the vulva will stimulate it and press and rub it against the pubic bone. Cupping the whole area with a hand or squeezing your palm down from the pubic bone can feel good. Some girls find direct touching of the exposed tip of the clitoris painful; some like the hood rubbed back and forth; some prefer to touch one side of the shaft of the clitoris rather than the other. You will discover what you enjoy best and, if you want to, you will be able to tell your sexual partner what turns you on. Some girls/women find that they can have an orgasm or several orgasms, quicker by direct clitoral stimulation than by vaginal intercourse. This does not mean that masturbation or direct clitoral stimulation by a partner is better or worse than intercourse; it's just different. You can prefer one or the other or like both.

Boys masturbate, or can be sexually stimulated by a partner, by rubbing the penis. Some like the whole hand wrapped round the penis and slid all the way up and down. Some like a thumb and two fingers placed just below the glans and pumped in short, quick movements. Some like to rub their penis between or against an object like a pillow. You will discover what you enjoy and, if you want to, you'll be able to show a sexual partner what turns you on.

If you are with a partner, you may like to rub your penis up and down between her breasts or between your partner's closed thighs or between the chest and arm while the arm is held down to the side. Take care not to ejaculate near a girl's vulva as some sperm can survive on the skin up to 72 hours and find their way into the vagina; for some positions it may be safer to use a condom.

AIDS Safety Rating: Solo masturbation – No Risk
Mutual Masturbation/Non-penetrative sexual stimulation – No Risk providing you have no open cuts or sores

SEX TOYS AND FINGER PENETRATION

Some girls and boys like to stroke themselves, touch their nipples and put their fingers inside their vagina and anus while solo masturbating or have their partner do these things in mutual masturbation or foreplay. Some people like to use sex toys to masturbate with, like vibrators or dildos. These are penis-shaped objects made of rubber or plastic, sometimes with a battery that makes them vibrate. They are used to stimulate the genitals and to insert inside the vagina or anus. Sex toys are expensive and some people improvise with penis-shaped objects, eg vegetables. If you use sex toys and/or insert your fingers into your own or your partner's vagina/anus:

1. Never put anything inside the vagina or anus that could damage it or tear the skin. A good rule is never to put anything there that you would not put in your mouth.
2. Take great care not to 'lose' a sex toy; once an object has passed the anal sphincter it can be very difficult to retrieve.
3. Anything placed inside the anus, whether it's fingers, a penis or a sex toy, *must not* then be placed inside your mouth or vagina. Bacteria which are perfectly healthy in the colon (the anal passage) can cause infections elsewhere.
4. *Never* use or let your partner use a sex toy without first thoroughly washing and drying it. HIV can be transmitted by sharing sex toys covered with the blood or genital secretions of an infected person.

AIDS Safety Rating: 1) Sex toys and/or insertion of fingers into the vagina or anus – No risk providing that the toys/ fingers are thoroughly washed and dried after each person and not shared.

2) Sharing sex toys with an infected person without sterilising them first – High Risk.

SEXUAL FANTASY

Some people like to fantasise while masturbating or to share fantasies with their sexual partner. This is fine as long as you're both happy about it.
AIDS Safety Rating: Sexual fantasy – No Risk

ORAL SEX

Oral sex means using your mouth to suck, kiss and lick your partner's sex organs. Most people find this idea rather startling at first. They feel shy about the smell and taste of their genital area. In fact clean sex organs smell and taste very exciting to a sexual partner. (Dirty sex organs, like smelly armpits and bad breath, smell awful.) You may enjoy washing or bathing together first as part of your sexual experience. Oral sex is common to hetero-sexual, gay and lesbian sex.

When oral sex is performed on a girl it's called cunnil-ingus. There are different positions in which it can be done, but the most common is for the partner to kneel between the girl's legs and lick and gently nibble the clitoris; the partner can also put their tongue into the girl's vagina and lightly brush the whole area.

When oral sex is performed on the boy, it's called fellatio. The partner sucks the penis by making a ring with their lips around the shaft and sliding it up and down. The partner may also fondle the balls or curve their hand around the bottom half of the penis. Alternatively, the partner can suck the top of the penis while rolling the shaft between their palms.

When partners perform oral sex at the same time it's called 69 or soixante-neuf (the French word for 69), probably because the two digits suggest two people lying next to each but in alternate positions.

If you have oral sex:

1. Remember that it could be dangerous to ejaculate into your partner's mouth when they are lying beneath you as they could choke on the semen.
2. It's fine to let your partner ejaculate into your mouth and/or to swallow his semen *as long as you are quite sure that he is not infected with HIV*. If you don't know whether your partner is infected or not or you are not sure, *do not allow him to ejaculate (come) in your mouth*. HIV is carried in the semen of people with HIV infection or AIDS.
3. *It is not safe to have oral sex with a girl who is menstruating unless you are sure she is not infected with HIV*. HIV is carried in menstrual blood. If you don't know whether your partner is infected or you're not sure, *do not have oral sex when she has her period*.
4. If you don't know whether your partner is infected with HIV or you're not sure, you should use a condom for oral sex. You can buy flavoured ones these days!
5. It is not thought possible to become infected with HIV from oral sex with a girl unless you have a cut or sore on your mouth (or unless she is menstruating).

AIDS Safety Rating: Oral sex with a boy – Medium Risk
Oral sex with a girl who is not menstruating – Low Risk
Oral sex with a girl who is menstruating – High Risk

Sexual Intercourse

There are two kinds of sexual intercourse – the one you'll probably have heard about is vaginal intercourse, which takes place between a girl and a boy. This is the most common form of heterosexual sex. The other kind is anal intercourse, which can take place between a girl and a boy or between two boys. Anal intercourse is a common form of homosexual sex.

Before sexual intercourse, partners stimulate each other's bodies by foreplay. This is necessary to prepare your body for intercourse. A girl's clitoris needs to be stimulated and the walls of her vagina need to produce the fluid which lubricates the vagina and vulva so that the penis can slide in without causing soreness. A boy's penis needs to be erect. With anal intercourse, KY jelly, Duragel or a lubricating spermicide should be used as there is no natural lubricant.

There are many positions in which sexual intercourse can take place; whichever way you both enjoy is good. The most common position for vaginal intercourse is for the girl to lie on her back with her legs open and knees bent. The boy lies on top of her and guides his penis into her vaginal opening; she can help by holding her vulva open. The couple then move their hips so that the penis slides backwards and forwards in the vagina. The walls of the vagina, the labia, the clitoris (indirectly) and the penis all stroke each other as they move, producing very intense and pleasurable feelings. These get more and more exciting until the partners reach orgasm. You can also have intercourse with the boy lying on his back and the girl on top, or standing up, or from behind, etc, etc.

The most common position for anal intercourse is for one partner to kneel on their knees and elbows while the other kneels directly behind and guides his lubricated penis into the anal opening. The couple then move their hips so that the penis slides backwards and forwards until orgasm is reached. Other positions are possible in much the same way as for vaginal intercourse.

For information about the law on vaginal and anal intercourse, see p 96 of this book. In vaginal intercourse it is also, of course, necessary to consider contraception *before* making love.

If you have sexual intercourse – *remember:*

If you don't know, or are not sure, whether your partner is free from HIV infection, *do not have vaginal or anal sex without using a condom.* The semen or vaginal fluid of an AIDS-infected person contains HIV. During intercourse there might be a break in the skin inside the vagina or anus or on the penis; it could be so small you won't feel it. If your partner is infected the virus could infect you through these small cuts. Anal intercourse is particularly risky because the anus is tight and dry and it is easier to tear the skin; choose an extra-strong condom and use KY jelly, Duragel or a spermicidal lubricant.
AIDS Safety Rating: Vaginal intercourse without a condom – High Risk
Anal intercourse without a condom – High Risk

ORGASM

When sexual tension and excitement build up to a high level we experience orgasm. This can happen in masturbation or in sexual activity with a partner. Many people have tried to describe orgasm; some say it's a rippling feeling which wells up and dies away again, or a soft rhythm in the genitals, or like an engulfing wave. Orgasm involves not just the body but the mind too – the whole being is caught up in an overwhelmingly intense and pleasurable sensation.

When a girl has an orgasm the walls of her vagina contract and she ejaculates fluid. A girl can sometimes have several orgasms in a row. When a boy has an orgasm he ejaculates and semen spurts from his penis. Once a boy has ejaculated, his penis goes limp and he has to wait at least half an hour before he can come again.

Sometimes one or both partners don't achieve orgasm when they make love. This is no big deal. The purpose of sexuality is pleasure and you can feel intense sexual pleasure just from engaging in sex with someone you like even if you don't reach orgasm. In fact you can ejaculate and not get much pleasure from it if you're not in the mood – it can feel rather mechanical. On the other hand you could just kiss and cuddle and get lots of pleasure and satisfaction. It's a mistake to think of everything you do in bed as steps that lead to orgasm. That would make it as though you were playing basketball and only enjoying scoring nets, not the rest of the game.

Some sex education books go on and on about the supreme moment of sexual achievement being when you come at the same time; it's as though that's something you're both supposed to work towards. Sure, it can be nice to come together, but it's also nice not to be preoccupied with your own orgasm and able to enjoy watching your partner have an orgasm. Try to experience each moment of a sexual encounter for the pleasure that the moment gives.

If you're sexually inexperienced (perhaps it's your first time), don't expect the earth to move. Who knows, perhaps it will, but first sexual experiences are usually clumsy and awkward. No matter how many books and magazines about sex you have read, doing it for real is something else. You'll probably be feeling nervous and tense. As I've said before, if you're having sex with someone you really like and care about, then the clumsiness and awkwardness won't matter so much – you'll both enjoy learning how to love each other at your own pace.

If you don't enjoy sex and/or have trouble having orgasms, it could be that you've been pushed into sex before you were ready and you should just give yourself a break. It could be that you don't know enough about your body and you've been rushing things – lots of nice cuddling, friendly petting and relaxed foreplay will help; masturbation may also help you to understand your own sexual needs and responses better. It could be that you've been made to feel guilty about sex; if you read more about it and talk with your friends, you'll realise what a natural and nice part of life it is. Perhaps you're uptight because you're frightened of getting pregnant or of HIV infection/ AIDS. If so, read p 77 and p 52 of this book and act on them.

For some boys, controlling ejaculation is sometimes a problem – a boy may find himself coming before he really wants to and before his partner has had time to enjoy the sexual experience. The most likely reason for this is anxiety. Perhaps you're making love in the back seat of a car and you're worried someone may walk past; perhaps you didn't get around to doing anything about contraception; perhaps you pretended to be a macho super-stud and you're scared your partner will realise that you're new to it all. Sort out problems like these if you can and then if you're still coming too soon, try this very simple yet effective technique: when you feel yourself tensing up, make sure that you are breathing deeply. Try to draw each breath past your lungs and deep into your body. You'll find that tension is then released by the deep breathing rather than by involuntary ejaculation.

If you're still unhappy about your sex life, try talking to your doctor or contact the organisations listed under *Counselling* on p 111 of this book.

SEX DRUGS

You may see 'sex drugs' on sale, in sex shops and other places, which claim to make you feel sexier and/or improve your performance. These drugs are stimulants based on amyl nitrate and they're highly dangerous, accounting for a proportion of teenage deaths from solvent abuse. They are known as 'poppers' and marketed under various brand names (eg 'Liquid Gold', 'Jungle Juice'). They're not just dangerous, they also do nothing for your sex life. Don't touch them.

SEX AND DISABILITY

If you are a person with disabilities, you may find that able-bodied people (parents, guardians, teachers, doctors) seem to assume that your sex life will be non-existent. Often they don't say anything at all, as if by ignoring your sexual feelings and needs they can make them go away. In the final section of this book I list organisations which do not take this view and which will help and advise you.

Some people with disabilities can never have 'spontaneous' sex because they need help in arranging their bodies comfortably and they need to explain what is painful and what isn't. You will have to learn, by listening to your body and learning about it, what your unique sexual response pattern is. A good way to do this, if you can, is to practise on yourself. Stroke and touch yourself, see what positions and what touches give you pleasure. What you discover about your body may be enough but if you need your sex life to include a sex partner, you will be able to convey this information about yourself to them.

If you are the sexual partner of a person with disabilities, you will for the most part, learn from them about what is happening with their body. But don't always leave it to them to explain things. Although they will have been dealing with the disability for a long time, sometimes it's good and supportive if you take the initiative and ask what s/he feels and would like.

Section 6
Contraception (Birth Control)

The only ways to make sure that a girl does not become pregnant are either not to have sex or to use a reliable method of contraception.

If you are having sex or planning to have sex, you must think about contraception beforehand. Girls have been known to get pregnant the very first time they make love. Some girls get pregnant because they and their partners feel too embarrassed to admit to themselves (and to each other) that they really are making love. They pretend that they only did it last time by mistake and they won't be doing it again, etc. Frankly, that's not very grown-up. You will almost certainly have a sexual relationship at some point in your life. Accept this about yourself. It's nothing to feel embarrassed about – *everyone* is a sexual person with sexual feelings and desires; in fact it would be a bit odd if we didn't all have such desires and feelings.

It takes two to make a baby. It's best if you and your partner can discuss contraception as a couple and support each other, whatever method you decide on. If you can't do this, then don't just hope that it's something your partner has thought about – do something about it yourself. Contraception is not a girl's responsibility or a boy's responsibility – it's the responsibility of each individual who risks causing an unwanted pregnancy.

Young people can get confidential advice on contraception from their GP, from the Family Planning Association and from Brook Advisory Centres. Some GPs will give advice but refuse to prescribe contraceptives for young people under 16 (although they can do so legally if they think your case is 'unusual'; see p 102). If this happens to you and it's a problem, go on trying to get help. The clinics listed at the back of the book will be able to advise you. Most doctors will help because they take the view that a young person who seeks advice on contraception is acting responsibly and maturely.

There are a lot of silly stories about ways of not getting pregnant – eg if you have sex standing up, or if you don't have an orgasm, or if it's the second time the boy ejaculates, or if you have a pee straight afterwards. None of these stories are true.

There are three preferable methods of contraception possible for young people – the pill, the diaphragm (plus a spermicide) and the condom. Of these three the most suitable and the most reliable is the pill. The other methods I discuss are either less suitable for young people or unreliable.

Contraception and AIDS

Do not confuse the need to protect yourself against AIDS with the need to use an effective contraceptive. The most reliable form of contraception is the pill; the most reliable way to protect yourself and your partner against HIV infection is to use a condom.

1. Girls who don't know or who are not sure whether their partner is free from HIV should continue to take the pill *and* should insist on their partner using a condom.
2. Girls who don't know or aren't sure whether they are free from HIV should continue to take the pill

(the babies of mothers infected by HIV can contract the disease) *and* should insist on their partner using a condom.

If you use a diaphragm, the coil, the pill, a spermicide, the rhythm method or withdrawal as methods of contraception *you are not protected against HIV.*

THE PILL (ORAL CONTRACEPTIVE)

The pill is a hormone pill that a girl swallows. It comes in a packet of 21 pills (usually) and you take one a day for three weeks, stop for seven days while you have your period, and then start a new pack. Each pack has full instructions. The pill either stops the ovum from being released from the ovary or it stops the fertilised egg from being implanted.

The pill is the most reliable form of birth control there is at the time of writing. It is particularly suitable for young sexually-active people as it frees you from thinking about contraception at the point of lovemaking. The pill is only available on prescription from your GP or clinic as it is not suitable for everyone. If you take the pill, do not smoke or you will increase your chance of thrombosis in later life.

The pill is no protection against AIDS. If you don't know or are not sure whether your partner is free from HIV, use a condom.

THE CONDOM (THE SHEATH, FRENCH LETTER, DUREX, RUBBER ETC)

The condom is a long rubber balloon rolled up in a packet. It is put on over a boy's erect penis. The condom stops the sperm getting spilt into the girl's vagina. Even before a boy comes, a small amount of semen can leak out of his penis and make the girl pregnant – that's why the condom must be put on before the penis comes into contact with the girl's sex organs. See p 61 for information about putting on and taking off a condom; this must be done carefully.

The advantages of the condom are that it is easy to use, it can be obtained free from Family Planning Clinics, it can be bought cheaply from chemists and other shops, it protects you and your partner from sexually transmitted diseases including AIDS, and it protects girls with a tendency to cervical cancer. Many couples find putting on a condom an exciting and erotic part of foreplay.

The disadvantage of the condom is that it can tear or break, especially if not properly put on. Ideally it should be used in conjunction with a spermicide for extra protection.

The Diaphragm plus Spermicide (Dutch Cap)

A diaphragm looks like a shallow bowl; the dome is made from thin rubber and the rim from wire covered with rubber. A girl inserts her diaphragm into her vagina so that it covers the cervix, stopping sperm reaching the ovum. The diaphragm must be used with a spermicide so that any sperm which manages to get past the diaphragm is killed by the spermicide. A diaphragm cannot disappear inside the vagina or get into your womb. It is easily inserted and easily removed. It is most suitable for girls with a regular partner who have their own flat or room.

The advantage of the diaphragm is that, if always used with a spermicide, it is a reliable method of birth control (a very small number of women using it get pregnant each year). It does not involve upsetting your hormone balance (like the pill) or setting up an infection in the womb (like the coil). During a period, the diaphragm will temporarily hold back the menstrual flow during sex. A diaphragm also protects girls with a tendency to cervical cancer.

The disadvantage of the diaphragm is that you have to remember to put it in before sex. It can be put in no more than three hours before intercourse after you have smeared spermicide on each side of the dome and around the rim. The diaphragm should not be removed after intercourse for at least six hours to be sure that all the sperm is killed. If you want to have intercourse again within the six hours, put in more spermicide (leaving the diaphragm in) and then wait for six hours after the *last* intercourse before removing it.

Not everyone's vagina is the same size or shape so you must go to a clinic to be individually fitted with a diaphragm. You will be taught how to put the diaphragm in by a doctor or nurse and how to apply spermicide. A diaphragm is rather springy but you'll soon get the knack. You must never borrow or lend a diaphragm – yours has been specially chosen to fit you. If you lose or gain a lot of weight (eg a stone) you may need to be refitted. After use, a diaphragm should be gently washed in warm soapy water, rinsed and dried very carefully. Check for tears by holding it up to the light; if you find any, take it back to the clinic and use alternative contraception in the meantime.

A diaphragm is no protection against AIDS. If you don't know or are not sure whether your partner is free from HIV, use a condom.

THE COIL (IUD)

The coil is a small wire and plastic device which is fitted

into the uterus (womb) by a doctor. The device comes in various shapes, eg the Nova T, the Multiload; it has a thread which hangs down into the vagina so that you can check it's still in place. The coil works by irritating the lining of the womb so that it will not accept a fertilised egg. Coils are not usually fitted in girls/women unless they have had a baby.

The advantage of the coil is that, once inserted, it can be left in place for at least three years. (When you have a bath you should check that you can still feel the thread in your vagina.) This means that you do not have to think about contraception at the point of lovemaking.

The disadvantage of the coil is that the womb may expel it (that's why you have to regularly check for the thread). It can also cause cramps and bleeding, especially just after it's been inserted. The coil has to be inserted and removed by a doctor. In some girls/women the coil can cause infections of the fallopian tubes – any pain or bleeding should be reported to your doctor at once. A very small number of women using the coil get pregnant.

A coil is no protection against AIDS. If you don't know or are not sure whether your partner is free from HIV, use a condom.

STERILISATION AND VASECTOMY

Sterilisation and vasectomy are operations which are usually irreversible so they are only carried out on adults who are quite sure that they don't want a child, or don't want another child.

In women, sterilisation involves clipping, cutting or burning the fallopian tubes so that no egg can reach the womb. In men, sterilisation is called 'vasectomy'; it involves cutting and tying the tubes in the testicles which carry sperm to the semen. The man can still ejaculate normally but his semen will not contain sperm.

Sterilisation and vasectomy are no protection against AIDS. If you don't know or are not sure whether your partner is free from HIV, use a condom.

WITHDRAWAL

Withdrawal means that the boy withdraws his penis from the girl's vagina before ejaculation, making sure that no sperm gets anywhere near her vagina. In fact, sperm can 'leak' from the penis before ejaculation, causing pregnancy. It is also very difficult for a boy to judge exactly when he is going to ejaculate. This method is *highly unreliable* and the cause of most unwanted teenage pregnancies. Sudden withdrawal can also spoil the sexual experience for both partners. If you are using this so-called method of contraception, you should seek advice about proper contraception at once from your doctor or clinic.
Withdrawal is no protection against AIDS. If you don't know or are not sure whether your partner is free from HIV, use a condom.

THE RHYTHM METHOD (THE 'SAFE PERIOD')

The Rhythm Method is the only birth-control method approved by thc Roman Catholic Church (some Catholics disagree and use the contraceptive methods already discussed). It involves trying to work out on which days a girl is likely to be fertile or infertile according to her menstrual cycle. To do this properly you need expert and individual advice from a clinic over a long period of time. Without this, it is not safe to assume that there is *any* day on which a girl can be absolutely sure that she will not get pregnant.

The Rhythm Method is no protection against AIDS. If you don't know or are not sure whether your partner is free from HIV, use a condom.

THE DOUCHE

You may read about douching in novels. It involved washing out the vagina immediately after intercourse with a special chemical or soapy water, which would be squeezed into the vagina by a rubber tube with a bulb on the end. This method did not work – in fact it would be more likely to push sperm up into the womb than wash it down. It also caused vaginal infections and could be highly dangerous. *Don't ever try it.* Of course it would be *no protection against AIDS.*

IF YOUR CONTRACEPTION FAILS (OR IF YOU WEREN'T USING ANY)

If a girl is involved in a contraceptive failure (eg a condom splits, you realise that your coil has fallen out) or if you weren't using any contraception or if you have been raped, you should go to your doctor immediately and request the post-coital pill. These pills must be taken within 72 hours of intercourse – your doctor will explain how many to take; they stop the fertilised egg, if there is one, being implanted. They will probably make you feel sick but this will not last long.

Another way of preventing implantation is to have a coil fitted within 7 days of having intercourse. Your doctor will advise on this.

If you fear that you may have become pregnant, it's sensible to go at once to your doctor for the post-coital pill or a coil, rather than wait until your next period is due to see whether or not you are pregnant. Your doctor will also be able to give you advice about reliable contraception for the future.

PREGNANCY TESTING

If you think you might be pregnant you should waste no time in finding out whether or not you are, by having a pregnancy test. A missed period may be a sign of pregnancy but it could just be that your cycle is irregular or even that fear of pregnancy is upsetting the cycle. You can have a pregnancy test done by your GP or at a clinic. You will need to take in a small sample of the first urine you pass in the morning. Thoroughly wash out a small jar with a lid (an old pill bottle would be ideal). You may have seen home pregnancy testing kits advertised; these are expensive and you must carry out the instructions carefully.

If you're not pregnant you need to ask yourself why you thought you were. Weren't you using a contraceptive? Do you need advice on contraception from a doctor or clinic? It's silly and irresponsible to put yourself through this panic every month.

ABORTION

If you are pregnant and don't want to have the baby, you must consult your doctor or clinic at once. They are experienced at dealing with young people in your position and will be able to help you to come to the right decision for you. If you are to have an abortion, then it is crucial not to delay in seeking advice. Delay will not only make the abortion medically more complicated, but at the time of writing there is increasing pressure on parliament to make abortion after 18 weeks illegal (at present abortion can be carried out up to 28 weeks). Remember too that once you have seen your doctor there may be delays at that end due to waiting lists. *If you think you may be pregnant and may want an abortion, go to your doctor at once.*

Do not try to abort yourself. Drinking gin in a hot bath will give you a hangover; jumping down the stairs may cause you to break your leg. Neither will cause an abortion. Do not be tempted to take mysterious medicines or pills or to have an illegal 'backstreet' abortion. Lots of girls and women used to do this before abortion was made legal in 1967, and lots died or were so seriously injured that they were later unable to have children when they wanted to. Statistics on deaths with an avoidable factor in 1964, 1965 and 1966 (just before abortion was legalised) reveal that just over one-third were associated with illegal abortion. The only safe abortion is the one arranged by your doctor or clinic.

It's unlikely that you will be able to handle all this on your own – you'll need support and help. Hopefully your boyfriend will be around to provide it since half the responsibility is his, but he may be the type who leaves you in the lurch. Your parents/guardians may freak out, but they may turn out to be surprisingly kind and understanding. There may be a sympathetic teacher at school you can turn to. Friends can be a great support – but beware of bad advice about gin bottles.

If you have an abortion, don't be surprised if you have mixed feelings afterwards. You'll feel relief that your life can now go on, but you may also have feelings of anger or sadness about what has happened. Allow yourself to feel sad while also realising that one day, if and when you want it, the time will be right for you to have a wanted baby in happy circumstances.

If you became pregnant because your contraception

failed or because you weren't using any, now is obviously the time to get all that put right by seeking advice from your doctor or clinic.

Having the Baby

If you think you want to have the baby, think very hard indeed. A baby is for life, whether you decide to put it up for adoption or whether you decide to keep it. Sometimes, of course, girls have no choice – they leave it too late to have an abortion even if they'd wanted one.

Adoption

If you decide to have the baby adopted you can feel confident that it will be well loved and cared for. These days there is a shortage of babies for adoption by people unable to have children of their own. Remember though that although adopted children now have the legal right to information about their biological parents, you do not have the legal right to information about a child you have given up for adoption. This can be very painful. Some parents who have given their children up for adoption have deposited letters and information with the Adoption Society so that the adopted child can easily trace them if s/he ever wants to. Your Adoption Society and social worker should be able to advise you on all this.

Keeping the Baby

It's simply not a good idea to get married or plan to live with someone just because you got pregnant by mistake. Such relationships rarely last and can cause resentment and bitterness. The most loving couple with a new baby which was planned find their relationship comes under strain after sleepless nights and when money is short. If you're thinking of keeping the baby, realistically you're likely to be bringing it up on your own. Some teenage girls do this and make a great job of it – but it's far from easy.

Even if you have the support and help of your parents/guardians you will almost inevitably find yourself facing financial difficulties and housing problems. It's not much fun in a hard-to-let flat on a run-down estate, which is all the council is likely to offer (and that's if you're lucky). If you live with your parents/guardians you'll at least have help with babysitting and looking after the baby, but you'll also have little control over the way you bring your child up. Unless your parents/guardians' home is large, you're likely too to suffer from overcrowding and the tension that that can generate. The worst problem for a teenage single mother, though, is loneliness – however wonderful your baby is, there will be times when you long for a night out with your friends.

Some girls think they would like to have a baby because they see it as a passport to the adult world and they don't have any other very clear idea of what the future could hold for them. And motherhood is certainly something that's sold to us all, all the time – women's magazines and television advertisements bombard us with images of happy smiling mummies with their adorable smiling babies. Babies *are* adorable, but what we're not shown are the realities of sleepless nights, nappy-changing, crying, your clothes with sick on them, and a baby's constant need for care and attention. All parents feel exhaustion and frustration some of the time.

Try to imagine what you'll be doing when you're thirty, and when you're forty and when you're fifty. Life as an adult lasts a long time, so make sure that you enjoy and benefit as much as possible from life as a teenager.

Section 7
Sexually Transmitted Diseases (STDs; VD)

The Special Clinic

If you suspect that you have a sexually transmitted disease (STD, also known as venereal disease or VD) it's important to get medical help as soon as possible. You can ring or go to your local hospital and ask for the 'Special Clinic' or look in the phonebook under VD – the phone number of your nearest Special Clinic will be listed. Of course your GP will be able to tell you where to go. A GP cannot treat you her/himself because specialist facilities are needed to diagnose STDs. You don't need a letter from your doctor or to be referred; you can just turn up. Diagnosis and treatment are confidential and free.

When you arrive at the Special Clinic you will be given a number of tests which will include taking smears and swabs, a blood sample and a urine sample. You will also be asked some details about your sex life. Tell the truth – doctors have heard it all before, and more, and are completely unshockable. They need the information so that they know how to treat you.

You will then either be asked to wait while the tests are analysed or to come back within the next two days. It is vital that you do return for the result of the tests. If you are infected, the disease could cause serious damage; you could also pass it on to someone else. If you have to return for treatment or more tests and take time off school or work, the Special Clinic will give you a doctor's certificate of attendance (which will not say what you're being treated for).

The Special Clinic may ask you to help them contact your sexual partner(s) who may also be infected and need treatment. This is to try and stop the spread of STDs. If you are in a position to let your partner(s) know yourself and persuade them to come for treatment, fine. If not, it's a good idea to let the Special Clinic handle it. They will do it very discreetly and they've had years of practice in tracing contacts. If you have one venereal disease, you need to be checked for others. Your partner(s) also need checking and possible treatment.

Of course you should not have sex until you are told that you are completely cured. Being cured once doesn't mean that you can't catch an STD again if you have sex with an infected person.

HIV INFECTION OR AIDS

AIDS is the most serious of the sexually transmitted diseases because, as yet, it cannot be cured although certain treatments are available. People who catch HIV may develop AIDS and then die. AIDS is discussed in detail elsewhere in this book. In the section 'Enjoying Sex' each sexual activity is also discussed in relation to HIV infection and AIDS and to safer sex.

GONORRHOEA

Gonorrhoea is the most common type of sexually transmitted disease. Gonorrhoea organisms are spread by sexual contact through vaginal, oral and anal intercourse.

Symptoms

In girls gonorrhoea is particularly dangerous because there are often no symptoms. You may get yellowish discharge from the vagina, and/or tummy pain. In boys, clear symptoms are usually present within a week. You get a thick, milky discharge from the penis and pain when peeing. These symptoms are similar to those of chlamydia so early diagnosis is vital, as is telling your partner to go for treatment.

Treatment

If gonorrhoea is not treated, it can spread to the internal sex organs, causing pain and sterility. Treatment is usually tablets of penicillin.

SYPHILIS (THE POX)

Syphilis is caused by a small spiral-shaped bacterium called a spirochaete. It is spread by sexual contact through vaginal, oral and anal sex.

Symptoms

The symptoms of syphilis are the same for girls and boys. They divide into four stages:

Stage 1. A painless sore called a chancre (pronounced 'shanker') appears on the genitals or the mouth. If it appears inside the anus or vagina or hidden in the folds of the vulva, it is often not noticed.

Stage 2. The bacteria spread through the body. A rash may appear and there may be a sore throat, fever or headache. Patches of hair may fall out.

Stage 3. During this stage which can last 10-20 years, there are no outwards signs but the bacteria may continue to damage the inner organs.

Stage 4. The syphilis may damage organs, causing blindness, paralysis, madness and death. (With modern medicine's ability to diagnose and treat syphilis this stage is rarely reached.)

Pregnant women with untreated syphilis can pass the disease into the bloodstream of the baby. This is why every pregnant woman is routinely tested for syphilis.

Treatment

Syphilis can be detected by a smear from a sore or by a blood test. Treatment is by penicillin injections or tetracycline.

Genital Herpes

Genital herpes is a viral disease spread by sexual intercourse with an infected person.

Symptoms

Sores which look like blisters or small bumps appear on the inside of the vagina, in or on the anus or on the penis. The blisters can rupture to form open sores which are painful and infectious to others.

Treatment

Creams and ointments are available to ease the discomfort. You are able to have sexual intercourse in between attacks without the likelihood of infecting your partner, but you must use a condom. Contact the organisation listed on p 115 for specialist advice *before* sexual activity.

Chlamydia

Chlamydia is a major cause of pelvic inflammatory disease and non-specific urethritis (NSU).

Symptoms
Many girls/women have no symptoms; some have unusual vaginal discharge. In boys the symptoms are similar to gonorrhoea – a thick milky discharge and pain when peeing.
Treatment
Tetracycline/Erythromium

TRICHOMONIASIS

Trichomoniasis or Trich is a one-celled protozoan found in boys and girls. It is usually sexually transmitted.
Symptoms
Girls with Trich have a yellowy-green discharge with a foul odour (also common in gonorrhoea). Boys with Trich often do not have symptoms.
Treatment
Metronidazole tablets by mouth. Both partners must be treated or you risk reinfecting each other.

YEAST INFECTIONS (THRUSH, CANDIDA, FUNGUS, MONILIA)

Candida albicans, a yeast fungus, grows normally in a girl's healthy vagina. When the system is thrown off balance (eg by antibiotics, by the pill, by feeling run-down) the yeast may grow profusely.
Symptoms
A thick white cheesy discharge which makes the vulva ache.
Treatment
A common home remedy is to wash the vagina daily with a solution of vinegar and warm water (¼ cup to 1 quart)

until the symptoms go away. Also coat a tampon with plain unsweetened yoghurt and put it in your vagina. These remedies should restore the natural balance in your vagina. If they do not work, your doctor will prescribe fungicidal pessaries and creams. A partner can also be infected and should be treated at the same time.

CYSTITIS

Cystitis is a very common infection of the bladder. It is not a venereal disease but may be associated with sexual activity. Nearly every girl/woman gets it at some point in her life. Infection can spread to the kidneys so early treatment is important.

Symptoms

The need to pee every few minutes although you don't have much to pee; a burning feeling when you do, and blood or pus in your water.

Treatment

A specimen of urine will be taken by your doctor to check for infection. Antibiotics will probably be prescribed. Drink a lot of water and pee frequently.

CRABS (PUBIC LICE, NITS)

Crabs are a form of lice which live on pubic hair; you can sometimes see the mites scurrying about. They lay eggs called nits (which look like black balls) at the roots of the hair. They are very itchy. You catch crabs by having sex or other physical contact with an infected person. (Don't share used underwear eg jock straps.)

Treatment

A lotion is available from chemists which will kill the crabs; you don't need to shave your pubic hair off. Follow the instructions carefully. Wash all bedding and clothing. Don't have sex until you're sure you are clear. If you have crabs, you must go to an STD clinic to be checked for other infections, as must your partner.

GENITAL WARTS

Warts on or near the sex organs are caused by a virus; they may look like ordinary skin warts, but not always. They can be sexually transmitted, (less than 20% are not sexually transmitted).

Treatment

The warts must be removed at a Special Clinic (STD Clinic). Don't try to do it yourself (the stuff sold in chemists for skin warts is *not* the right treatment). If your partner is not treated at the same time you may catch them again. The STD Clinic will advise you about using condoms.

SECTION 8
SEX AND THE LAW

Laws are made either to protect us (eg from thieves, from speeding motorists) or to express society's disapproval of particular kinds of behaviour. In Britain many of the laws which govern sexual behaviour reflect views (eg that homosexuality is wrong, that females are the property of males) that many people now consider to be wrong and to be an interference in the lives of people who are not harming themselves or anyone else.

At the same time it is important that people, particularly children and young people, should be protected from unwanted sexual attention from those who are more powerful than they are. Even here the law is sometimes an ass (eg boys under 14 cannot be prosecuted for rape as the law does not consider them physically capable of the act) and the conduct of, for example, child abuse cases is currently a great cause for concern.

INCEST AND ABUSE OF CARE

In Britain you are not allowed to marry or have sexual intercourse with your father, mother, step-father, step-mother, grandmother, grandfather, uncle, aunt, step-brother, step-sister, brother or sister. You can marry and have a sexual relationship with your cousins, including first cousins.

Sexual acts which do not amount to sexual intercourse (eg touching of the genitals, oral sex) are not classified as incest but are also illegal. They would be considered indecent assault.

The most common form of incest is a sexual relationship between a father and a daughter, but it can also be between a father and son, a brother and sister, a grandfather and granddaughter, a brother and brother, a mother and son etc.

Some adults are in the position of being parents although they are not biological parents (eg your Mum's live-in boyfriend, your foster-father, the staff of your children's home, your teacher) and they therefore have the kind of responsibilities that parents have towards the children in their care. It is illegal for them to abuse that care and form a sexual relationship with you; they can be prosecuted for indecent assault and/or rape.

Incest, sexual assault and abuse of care are crimes against the child or young person. The person responsible is always the adult or older person who ought to know better. If this is happening, or has happened to you, try telling a sympathetic adult you can trust – a teacher, a doctor, a relative in whom you have confidence. If you have no one to tell or you are not believed, contact the organisations listed at the end of this book. They will believe you and will offer help and support.

THE AGE OF CONSENT (SEX BETWEEN MALES AND FEMALES)

It is illegal for a boy or man to have sexual intercourse or any other kind of sexual intimacy with a girl under 16. This is known as the age of consent. (In Northern Ireland it is 17 and in the Republic of Ireland 18.) But a girl/woman cannot be prosecuted for unlawful sexual intercourse if she has sex with boys of any age, including under 16. If the boy is under 16 she *could* be prosecuted for indecent assault.

GIRLS AND WOMEN IN HETEROSEXUAL RELATIONSHIPS

Girls and women cannot be prosecuted for having sex at any age apart from incest or indecent assault on a boy under 16, or for being involved in prostitution.

BOYS AND MEN IN HETEROSEXUAL RELATIONSHIPS

1. If you are under 14 you cannot be charged with 'unlawful sexual intercourse' (having sex with a girl who is under age) or with rape. You can be charged with indecent assault even if she consented, but this charge is rarely brought unless you have attacked a girl/woman.
2. If you are 14 or over and have sex with a girl under 16 you can be charged with 'unlawful sexual intercourse'. In practice, there are very few prosecutions of boys under 17.
3. If you are 17 or over and have sex with a girl under 16 you could be sent to prison for up to two years, or longer if the girl was under 13.
4. If you and your girlfriend live together and she is under 16, you could be charged with taking an unmarried girl away from her parents, even if you don't have sex. If you are 17 or over and are convicted you could be sent to prison for up to two years. In practice there are few prosecutions of this kind.

5. Boys under 16 can be asked to contribute to a child's upkeep if they father a child.

IF YOU ARE PROSECUTED

Lots of young people have sexual relationships when either or both partners are under 16 without realising that they are breaking the law. Usually the law does not interfere. But a case could be brought against you if your parents/guardians were to object or if you are under a social worker who thinks that you are in 'moral danger'. The grounds of 'moral danger' are sometimes used to take young people into care if the social worker thinks that you are promiscuous or becoming involved in prostitution. If you need legal help you should contact the organisations listed at the back of this book.

ANAL INTERCOURSE BETWEEN HETEROSEXUALS

Many couples have anal intercourse (buggery, sodomy) – the penis is put into the anus – without ever realising that it's illegal. For a prosecution to be brought a girl/woman would have to make a complaint to the police about her partner.

SAME-SEX RELATIONSHIPS

The law still discriminates against gay people. Gay men are denied equality with heterosexual men; lesbian mothers are often denied custody of their children because they are lesbian. If you are in the armed forces you will probably be asked to leave if it is discovered that you are gay or lesbian. If you are a gay man in the armed forces you can be court-martialled if you are discovered to be having a sexual relationship, even if you are over 21.

Girls and Women in Lesbian Relationships

Lesbian relationships are not recognised in law and have never been illegal (apart from in the armed forces). There was an attempt to introduce a law against lesbian relationships in 1920 but it was thought that it might put ideas into women's heads. If you are both over 16 your relationship is lawful. If one partner is over 16 and the other is not, it would be possible to prosecute on the grounds of indecent assault or gross indecency but in practice this hardly ever happens.

Boys and Men in Homosexual (Gay) Relationships

The law discriminates against gay men and boys. Although heterosexuals and lesbians can have sexual intercourse legally from the age of 16, gay men cannot have sexual relationships legally until they are 21. In the armed forces gay sexual relationships are illegal even for men over 21. In fact many gays either don't know about or ignore the law and do not come to the attention of the police. But you should know what the legal position is.

It is illegal for you to have a sexual relationship with a boy or man unless you are both 21 or over. The relationship is then only legal if it takes place between two individuals, if you both consent, if it takes place in private, and if you are not in the armed forces.

If you are involved in homosexual relationships illegally you could be charged with:

1 Buggery. This means anal intercourse (sodomy). Buggery is an offence if one or both of you are under 21, if one partner does not consent, if the act is not in private or if you are in the army. You could also be charged if your partner was 'severely abnormal'.
2 Gross indecency. This covers any homosexual act between males other than anal intercourse (eg mutual masturbation). It is most often used when the police say that the act was not in private (eg in public lavatories, in a park) or if one of you is under 21.
3 Indecent assault. A man can be charged with indecent assault if his partner is under 16 or if his partner is 16 or over but did not consent. 'Indecent assault' can mean anything from anal intercourse to touching.
4 Importuning. If you repeatedly try to pick up another boy or man in a public place or if you approach more than one boy/man, you can be charged with soliciting or importuning. In practice the police arrest people for this at well-known pick-up places.

When Can You be Charged With a Homosexual Offence?

1 If you are under 14 you cannot be prosecuted for buggery (anal intercourse) but you could be prosecuted for indecent assault.
2 If you are under 16 the law assumes (as it does for girls under 16) that you are incapable of

consenting to a homosexual relationship. If you have sex or any other kind of intimacy with someone who is under 16, or with someone who is older but who does not consent, you could be prosecuted for indecent assault. If your partner is 16 or over, he could be prosecuted for indecently assaulting you or for buggery, even if you consented.

3 If you are under 17 you could be taken into care or placed under a supervision order (a social worker keeps an eye on you while you go on living at home) because of your homosexual relationship.

4 If you are 16 or over both you and your partner could be prosecuted for gross indecency or buggery (anal intercourse). This happens rarely.

If You Are Arrested

If you are arrested you can refuse to answer police questions and refuse to be medically examined. You should ask to contact your solicitor or legal advice centre (see the back of the book for organisations to contact).

CONTRACEPTION AND THE LAW

If you are having a sexual relationship you need advice on contraception. If you are under 16 your doctor or clinic will advise you and prescribe contraception without your parents being told or asked for their permission if the doctor feels that your case is 'unusual'. Your case will be considered 'unusual' if:

- you really don't feel able to tell your parents/guardians

- it's best for you to get advice and treatment although your parents/guardians don't know
- you understand the advice you're asking for
- you're likely to have sex without contraception
- you're likely to suffer physically and mentally if you don't get advice and treatment

The doctor will decide whether you can consent to the treatment (this means s/he thinks you capable of understanding it) and whether it is in your interest to prescribe contraception.

If you are 16 or over, you are entitled to advice on contraception and treatment and it's up to you whether you tell your parents/guardians or not. There is no law that they should know. Contraceptives from Family Planning Clinics or on prescription are free.

None of this applies in the Republic of Ireland, where it is illegal to advise or prescribe contraception for unmarried people.

ABORTION AND THE LAW

An abortion needs the consent of two doctors, which can cause delays, so go to your doctor at once if you think you may be pregnant and may need an abortion. If your doctor is against abortion (eg s/he may be Roman Catholic) you should immediately contact one of the advice agencies listed in Section 9 of this book. If you are under 16, the law now requires your doctor to inform your parents. *Do not let this deter you from seeking early advice.* Your doctor will have dealt with many young people in your situation and be able to advise you.

MARRIAGE

You cannot get married until you are 16. If you are 16 or

17 you need the written permission of your parents/legal guardians (or the local council if you are in care) to marry in a registry office. If you marry in church you don't need written permission but the banns must be read for three consecutive Sundays. In Scotland you don't need any permission once you are 16. If your parents/guardians refuse to consent to your marriage you can apply to the local Country Court for permission. If you try to get married without your parents/guardians' consent, you could be made a ward of court. The court would then decide whether you can marry.

LIVING TOGETHER

Once you are 18 you can live where and with whom you want to. If you are under 18 you can live together as long as your parents/guardians don't object. If they do object they could stop you by having you made a ward of court, or by complaining to the police or local social services; this could result in your being taken into care.

RAPE AND INDECENT ASSAULT

A man or boy aged 14 or over who has sexual intercourse with a girl/woman who does not consent has committed rape. Rape is legally defined as penetration by the penis of the vagina. If the girl/woman submits to intercourse because of threats or because she has been given drink or drugs, the man/boy can also be found guilty of rape. A boy under 14 cannot be prosecuted for rape but he could be prosecuted for indecent assault.

Other forms of sexual assault which do not involve the penetration of the vagina by the penis (eg forced oral sex) can be quite as horrific as rape. Charges of indecent assault or grievous bodily harm can be brought.

Women and girls do sometimes carry out sexual assaults, but the vast majority of such crimes are committed by men and boys – on other men and boys as well as on girls and women.

If you are the victim of rape or sexual assault you will need help and support while you recover. You may decide to report the rape/assault to the police. If you do, you should do so as soon as you are able, as your appearance and behaviour following the attack will be used by the police as part of the evidence that you were attacked. One of your first reactions will be to want to wash away all traces of your attacker – but by doing this you will be destroying vital evidence. Until you have had a chance to decide whether to report the rape/attack or not:

- do not wash or bath
- do not change or throw away the clothes you were wearing when attacked
- do not drink alcohol or take drugs

Whether you report the rape/assault or not, you should contact the organisations listed in Section 9, who offer advice and support to victims of sexual attack. Being attacked in this way is a heavy burden to carry; these organisations will help you to come to terms with it.

Prostitution

Prostitution is selling sex for money. Both women and men can be prostitutes – female prostitutes are also called 'call-girls' and male prostitutes 'rent-boys'. Men who control and live off the earnings of prostitution are called pimps.

Sometimes teenagers get caught up in prostitution. There can be many reasons – perhaps your home life is unbearable and sex with strangers offers you affection and comfort of a sort; perhaps you think it's an easy way to make money; perhaps you desperately need money because you're hooked on drugs; perhaps you've run away from home and you can't make ends meet.

If you are involved in prostitution now, it doesn't mean that you will be always. There are agencies who will help you think about what you're doing and help you to get out of it. If your problem is drug dependency or homelessness, there are organisations listed at the back of this book which will help with this too. But you *must* get out of it. Selling sex is extremely dangerous. People who do it risk murder, brutal assault, torture, being drawn into pornography, catching sexually transmitted diseases including AIDS, and possible future difficulties in relating to someone they love.

AIDS AND YOUR RIGHTS

No one (including young people) can be tested for HIV if they don't want to be. This applies to all young people including those in care or in custody. If you do decide to be tested you have the right to precounselling and you must be able to give your 'informed consent' to the test. This ruling is from the British Medical Association and these procedures are agreed by the Home Office and the Prison Department.

BESTIALITY

Bestiality means sex with animals. It's far from common but it does happen. It's quite impossible for a woman to become pregnant by an animal or for an animal to become pregnant by a man. Vaginal or anal intercourse with an animal is illegal.

TRANSVESTISM (CROSS-DRESSING)

Transvestites are people (usually men) who like to dress up in the clothes of the opposite sex. Some only do this in private, some like to go out dressed in this way. Some heterosexuals are cross-dressers and some homosexuals are cross-dressers; transvestism is not necessarily related to sexual behaviour.

PAEDOPHILIA

Paedophiles are people who are sexually attracted to children. It is quite illegal to have sexual intercourse or any kind of sexual intimacy with children. If this has happened or is happening to you, contact the organisations listed in the back of this book, who will advise and help you.

SECTION 9
WHERE TO GET HELP AND ADVICE

When you need help, try to talk to someone you trust – perhaps your parents/guardians, your teacher or your doctor. If you don't have anyone you can talk to, contact the organisations listed here. Many of them are in London, but some have branches in different parts of the country that they can put you in touch with. Most will deal with callers from outside London. London numbers start with 01. If you are in London do not dial the 01, just the rest of the number.

Abortion – see Contraception

Abuse of Care – see Incest

AIDS/HIV Infection

For information and advice on all aspects of AIDS/HIV infection contact:

The Terence Higgins Trust
BM/AIDS
London WC1N 3XX
which has a wide range of leaflets free on request.

The Terence Higgins Trust Helpline:

(01) 833 2971 7pm-10pm weekdays
3pm-10pm weekends

The National Advisory Service on AIDS
Helpline: 0800 567123 Freecall 24 hrs

Welsh AIDS Campaign
Helpline: 0222 464121

Northern Ireland AIDS line
Helpline: 0232 226117

Scottish AIDS Monitor
Helpline: 041 221 7467

Your local STD (VD) clinic. Advice is free and confidential. Look in the phone book under Sexually Transmitted Diseases (STDs) or Venereal Disease (VD) for the phone number and address of your nearest clinic. You don't have to be referred by your doctor, you can just turn up.

Lesbian and Gay Switchboard will discuss AIDS/HIV infection and put you in touch with local support groups
(01) 837 7324

The Health Education Council,
78 New Oxford, Street,
London WC1A 1AH
(01) 631 0930
produces booklets on AIDS and has a reference library of all such publications

Body Positive Group
(01) 837 7324

offers advice to those who have HIV infection

FACT (Facilitators for AIDS Co-ordination and Training),
48b Rossiter Road
Balham
London SW12 9RU
(01) 274 2289
offers training on AIDS/HIV infection to youth workers and teachers on issues to do with young people and AIDS/HIV.

AIDS/HIV infection Helplines in Australia:
Sydney – AIDS Hotline: (02) 332 4000
Melbourne – AIDS line: (03) 419 3166

AIDS/HIV infection Helplines in Canada:
Toronto – AIDS Hotline: (416) 926 1626

AIDS/HIV infection Helplines in New Zealand:
Auckland – AIDS Foundation New Zealand: (9) 395560

Being Arrested – see **Legal Rights**

Bi-Sexuality – see **Gay and Lesbian Advice Organisations**

Childline

This is a national help and advice service for children and young people.

Childline
Freepost 1111 (no stamp needed)
London EC4 4BB
phone number 0800 1111 (the number is the same wherever you live; the service is free and open 24 hrs)

The Childline phone service is so busy that it's often difficult to get through. For some problems Childline cannot help you directly but will refer you to some of the other specialist organisations listed here.

Contraception

For advice on contraception, abortion or pregnancy counselling contact:

British Pregnancy Advisory Service (BPAS)
7 Belgrave Road
London SW1V 1QB
(01) 222 0985

Brook Advisory Centres
153a East Street
London SE17 2SD
(01) 708 1234

Family Planning Association
27 Mortimer Street
London W1N 7RJ
(01) 636 7866

Counselling

The following organisations offer sympathetic and impartial counselling on family and other problems:

Family Network Services
National Children's Home (NCH)
Stephenson Hall
85c Highbury Park
London N5 1UD

Regional telephone numbers for this organisation:
Birmingham (021) 440 5970
Cardiff (0222) 29461
Glasgow (041) 2216722
Glenrothes (0592) 759651
Gloucester (0452) 24019
Leeds (0532) 456456
London (01) 514 1177
Luton (052) 422751
Maidstone (0622) 56677
Manchester (061) 2369873
Norwich (0603) 660679
Preston (0772) 24006
Swansea (0792) 292798
Taunton (0823) 73191

National Association of Young People's
Counselling and Advisory Services
(NAYPCAS)
17-23 Albion Street
Leicester LE1 6GD
(0533) 554775

Teenage Information Network (TIN)
102 Harper Road
London SE1 6AQ
(01) 403 2444 (London only)

Depression and Despair

Contact the organisations listed in **Counselling.** If

things are really bad ring the Samaritans. You will find the local number in the phone book or you can ask the operator to put you through directly. This is a 24hr service.

Disability and Sex

For advice and information contact:

S.P.O.D. (Sexual Problems of the Disabled)
286 Camden Road
London N7 0BJ
(01) 607 8851

The Disabled Living Foundation
380 Harrow Road
London W9
(01) 289 6111

RADAR (Royal Association for Disability and Rehabilitation)
25 Mortimer Street
London W1N 8AB
(01) 637 5400

Drugs

For help with a drugs problem contact:

Standing Conference on Drug Abuse (SCODA)
Kingsbury House
1-4 Hatton Place
Hatton Garden
London EC1N 8ND
(01) 430 2341

Community Drug Project
30 Manor Place
London SE17 3BB
(01) 703 0559 (London only)

Families Anonymous
88 Caledonian Road
London N1 9ND
(01) 278 8805 (London only)

Gay and Lesbian Advice Organisations

For information and advice on being gay, lesbian or bi-sexual contact:

Lesbian and Gay Switchboard
BM Switchboard
London WC1N 3XX
(01) 837 7324

Lesbian and Gay Switchboard can put you in touch with organisations which specialise in helping young gay and lesbian people 'come out' to their parents, and can put parents in touch with support groups such as:

Parents Anonymous
(01) 668 4805 24hrs

National Friend
BM National Friend
London WC1N 3XX
(01) 837 3337
will also advise young people on bi-sexuality

Lesbian and Gay Youth Movement
LGYM BM GYM

London WC1N 3XX
(01) 319 9690

This is a national organisation for young people which provides advice and help, runs a penfriends' scheme and annual festivals and publishes a Gay Youth magazine.

Lesbian Line
BM Box 1514
London WC1N 3XX
(01) 251 6911

Haemophilia

For help and advice for people with haemophilia and on haemophilia and HIV infection/AIDS;

The Haemophilia Society
16 Trinity Street
London SE1 1DE
(01) 407 1010

Health Education

The Health Education Council produces leaflets on all aspects of health education and has an extensive reference library:

The Health Education Council
78 New Oxford Street
London WC1A 1AH
(01) 631 0930

Herpes

For help and advice for people with herpes:

The Herpes Association
41 North Road
London N7
(01) 609 9061

Advice can also be obtained from your nearest STD (VD) clinic.

HIV Infection – see AIDS

Incest/Abuse of Care

The following organisations will be able to contact someone in your area who will help you to deal with the situation and find you a place of safety:

The National Society for the Prevention of Cruelty to Children (NSPCC)
(branches in England, Wales and Northern Ireland)
67 Saffron Hill
London EC1N 8RS
(01) 242 1626

Royal Scottish Society for the Prevention of Cruelty to Children
Melville House
41 Polworth Terrace
Edinburgh EH11 1NU
(031) 337 8539/8530

The Church of England Children's Society
Edward Rudolf House
Margery Street
London WC1X 0JL
(01) 837 4299

(You don't have to be Church of England to contact this organisation)

Touchline (for people in the Yorkshire area) (0532) 457777

Incest Crisis Line
32 Newbury Close
Northolt
Middlesex UB5 4JF

This service is run by incest survivors:
Richard (01) 422 5100
Shirley (01) 890 4732
Anne (01) 302 0570
Petra (Southend-on-Sea) (0702) 584 702
Chris (Carlisle) (0965) 31432

Incest Survivors Campaign
London: (01) 852 7432
(01) 737 1354
Manchester (061) 236 1712
Dundee (0382) 21545
Belfast (0232) 249 696

Avon Sexual Abuse Centre (for people in the Avon area)
39 Jamaica Street
Stokes Croft
Bristol BS2 8JP
(0272) 428331

Black Women's Campaign Against Child Sexual Abuse
Black Women's Centre
(01) 274 9220

Taboo (for people in the Manchester area)
PO Box 38
Manchester M60 1HG
(061) 236 1323

Choices (for people in the Cambridge area)
(0223) 314438

Australia

Canberra
Children's Services – (062) 462625 (9am to 5pm)
Sydney
Child Protection and Family Crisis – (02) 818 5555 (24 hours)
2UE Kids Careline – (02) 929 7799 (9am to 5pm, Mon-Fri)
Darwin
Department for Community Development – (089) 814 733
Brisbane
Crisis Care – (07) 224 6855 (24 hours)
Adelaide
Crisis Care – (08) 272 1222 (24 hours)
Hobart
Department of Community Welfare, Crisis Intervention (002) 302 529 (24 hours)
Melbourne
Protective Services for Children – (03) 309 5700 (9am to 5pm)
Perth
Crisis Care – (09) 321 4144 (24 hours) or (008) 199 008 (toll free)

You can also contact through your local directory:
The Police
Lifeline
Rape Crisis Centres

New Zealand
Auckland
Help – 399 185 (24 hours)

Canada
The emergency number in Canada is 911.
For help and/or advice:
- Look in the telephone directory on the first page under Child Abuse
- Ring the police or social services

or
- Contact: National Clearinghouse on Family Violence
Health & Welfare Canada
Ottawa
Ontario K1A 1B5
(613) 9572938

who will refer you to someone in your area.

Legal Rights

The Children's Legal Centre
20 Compton Terrace
London N1 2UN
(01) 359 6251

National Council for Civil Liberties (NCCL)
21 Tabard Street
London SE1 4LA
(01) 403 3888

Release,
169 Commercial Street
London E1 6BW
Emergency (24 hrs): (01) 603 8654
for information and help in dealing with the Police, the Criminal Courts or drugs problems.

Lesbianism – see **Gay and Lesbian**

Pregnancy – see **Contraception**

Prostitution

At the time of writing there is only one organisation which specialises in helping young people caught up in prostitution:

Streetwise
PO Box 185
London SW5 9JR
(01) 373 8860

but the organisations listed under **Counselling** will also offer help and advice.

Rape/Sexual Assault

For girls and women:

The Rape Crisis Centre
PO Box 69
London WC1X 9NJ
(01) 837 1600 (24 hrs)
The number of your nearest Rape Crisis Centre should be in the phone book.

For gay men and boys there is no equivalent to the Rape Crisis Centre but help and advice can be obtained from:

Lesbian and Gay Switchboard
BM Switchboard
London WC1N 3XX
(01) 837 7324

National Friend
BM National Friend
London WC1N 3XX
(01) 837 3337

For heterosexual men and boys there is no equivalent to the Rape Crisis Centre. Help and advice can be obtained from the organisations listed under **Counselling**.

If you want to contact the police ring 999 or your local police station (number in the phone book).

For support and counselling in the long term:
The Victim Aid Scheme
(01) 729 1252

Sexual Assault – see Rape

Sexually Transmitted Diseases

If you suspect that you have a sexually transmitted disease it's important to get help as soon as possible. Ring your local hospital or look in the phone book under Sexually Transmitted Diseases (STDs) or Venereal Disease (VD) for the address of your nearest clinic. See also **AIDS/HIV Infection**.

Index